Life Application Bible Studies
1 & 2 TIMOTHY / TITUS

APPLICATION® BIBLE STUDIES

Part 1:
Complete text of 1 & 2 Timothy / Titus with study notes and features from the *Life Application Study Bible*

Part 2:
Thirteen lessons for individual or group study

Study questions written and edited by

Rev. David R. Veerman
Dr. James C. Galvin
Dr. Bruce B. Barton

New Living Translation®

Tyndale House Publishers, Inc.
Carol Stream, Illinois

Visit Tyndale's exciting Web sites at www.newlivingtranslation.com and www.tyndale.com.

New Living Translation, NLT, the New Living Translation logo, and *Life Application* are registered trademarks of Tyndale House Publishers, Inc.

Life Application Bible Studies: 1 & 2 Timothy / Titus

Copyright © 1998, 2010 by Tyndale House Publishers, Inc., Carol Stream, Illinois 60188. All rights reserved.

Life Application notes and features copyright © 1988, 1989, 1990, 1991, 1993, 1996, 2004 by Tyndale House Publishers, Inc., Carol Stream, Illinois 60188. Maps in text copyright © 1986, 1988 by Tyndale House Publishers, Inc. All rights reserved.

Cover photograph copyright © by Corbis. All rights reserved.

The text of 1 & 2 Timothy and Titus is from the *Holy Bible,* New Living Translation, copyright © 1996, 2004, 2007 by Tyndale House Foundation. All rights reserved.

ISBN 978-1-4143-2652-8

Printed in the United States of America

26 25 24 23 22 21 20
8   7   6   5   4   3   2

CONTENTS

A NOTE TO READERS

The *Holy Bible,* New Living Translation, was first published in 1996. It quickly became one of the most popular Bible translations in the English-speaking world. While the NLT's influence was rapidly growing, the Bible Translation Committee determined that an additional investment in scholarly review and text refinement could make it even better. So shortly after its initial publication, the committee began an eight-year process with the purpose of increasing the level of the NLT's precision without sacrificing its easy-to-understand quality. This second-generation text was completed in 2004 and is reflected in this edition of the New Living Translation. An additional update with minor changes was subsequently introduced in 2007.

The goal of any Bible translation is to convey the meaning and content of the ancient Hebrew, Aramaic, and Greek texts as accurately as possible to contemporary readers. The challenge for our translators was to create a text that would communicate as clearly and powerfully to today's readers as the original texts did to readers and listeners in the ancient biblical world. The resulting translation is easy to read and understand, while also accurately communicating the meaning and content of the original biblical texts. The NLT is a general-purpose text especially good for study, devotional reading, and reading aloud in worship services.

We believe that the New Living Translation—which combines the latest biblical scholarship with a clear, dynamic writing style—will communicate God's word powerfully to all who read it. We publish it with the prayer that God will use it to speak his timeless truth to the church and the world in a fresh, new way.

The Publishers
October 2007

INTRODUCTION TO THE
NEW LIVING TRANSLATION

Translation Philosophy and Methodology

English Bible translations tend to be governed by one of two general translation theories. The first theory has been called "formal-equivalence," "literal," or "word-for-word" translation. According to this theory, the translator attempts to render each word of the original language into English and seeks to preserve the original syntax and sentence structure as much as possible in translation. The second theory has been called "dynamic-equivalence," "functional-equivalence," or "thought-for-thought" translation. The goal of this translation theory is to produce in English the closest natural equivalent of the message expressed by the original-language text, both in meaning and in style.

Both of these translation theories have their strengths. A formal-equivalence translation preserves aspects of the original text—including ancient idioms, term consistency, and original-language syntax—that are valuable for scholars and professional study. It allows a reader to trace formal elements of the original-language text through the English translation. A dynamic-equivalence translation, on the other hand, focuses on translating the message of the original-language text. It ensures that the meaning of the text is readily apparent to the contemporary reader. This allows the message to come through with immediacy, without requiring the reader to struggle with foreign idioms and awkward syntax. It also facilitates serious study of the text's message and clarity in both devotional and public reading.

The pure application of either of these translation philosophies would create translations at opposite ends of the translation spectrum. But in reality, all translations contain a mixture of these two philosophies. A purely formal-equivalence translation would be unintelligible in English, and a purely dynamic-equivalence translation would risk being unfaithful to the original. That is why translations shaped by dynamic-equivalence theory are usually quite literal when the original text is relatively clear, and the translations shaped by formal-equivalence theory are sometimes quite dynamic when the original text is obscure.

The translators of the New Living Translation set out to render the message of the original texts of Scripture into clear, contemporary English. As they did so, they kept the concerns of both formal-equivalence and dynamic-equivalence in mind. On the one hand, they translated as simply and literally as possible when that approach yielded an accurate, clear, and natural English text. Many words and phrases were rendered literally and consistently into English, preserving essential literary and rhetorical devices, ancient metaphors, and word choices that give structure to the text and provide echoes of meaning from one passage to the next.

On the other hand, the translators rendered the message more dynamically when the literal rendering was hard to understand, was misleading, or yielded archaic or foreign wording. They clarified difficult metaphors and terms to aid in the reader's understanding. The translators first struggled with the meaning of the words and phrases in the ancient context; then they rendered the message into clear, natural English. Their goal was to be both faithful to the ancient texts and eminently readable. The result is a translation that is both exegetically accurate and idiomatically powerful.

Translation Process and Team

To produce an accurate translation of the Bible into contemporary English, the translation team needed the skills necessary to enter into the thought patterns of the ancient authors and then to render their ideas, connotations, and effects into clear, contemporary English.

To begin this process, qualified biblical scholars were needed to interpret the meaning of the original text and to check it against our base English translation. In order to guard against personal and theological biases, the scholars needed to represent a diverse group of evangelicals who would employ the best exegetical tools. Then to work alongside the scholars, skilled English stylists were needed to shape the text into clear, contemporary English.

With these concerns in mind, the Bible Translation Committee recruited teams of scholars that represented a broad spectrum of denominations, theological perspectives, and backgrounds within the worldwide evangelical community. Each book of the Bible was assigned to three different scholars with proven expertise in the book or group of books to be reviewed. Each of these scholars made a thorough review of a base translation and submitted suggested revisions to the appropriate Senior Translator. The Senior Translator then reviewed and summarized these suggestions and proposed a first-draft revision of the base text. This draft served as the basis for several additional phases of exegetical and stylistic committee review. Then the Bible Translation Committee jointly reviewed and approved every verse of the final translation.

Throughout the translation and editing process, the Senior Translators and their scholar teams were given a chance to review the editing done by the team of stylists. This ensured that exegetical errors would not be introduced late in the process and that the entire Bible Translation Committee was happy with the final result. By choosing a team of qualified scholars and skilled stylists and by setting up a process that allowed their interaction throughout the process, the New Living Translation has been refined to preserve the essential formal elements of the original biblical texts, while also creating a clear, understandable English text.

The New Living Translation was first published in 1996. Shortly after its initial publication, the Bible Translation Committee began a process of further committee review and translation refinement. The purpose of this continued revision was to increase the level of precision without sacrificing the text's easy-to-understand quality. This second-edition text was completed in 2004, and an additional update with minor changes was subsequently introduced in 2007. This printing of the New Living Translation reflects the updated 2007 text.

Written to Be Read Aloud
It is evident in Scripture that the biblical documents were written to be read aloud, often in public worship (see Nehemiah 8; Luke 4:16-20; 1 Timothy 4:13; Revelation 1:3). It is still the case today that more people will hear the Bible read aloud in church than are likely to read it for themselves. Therefore, a new translation must communicate with clarity and power when it is read publicly. Clarity was a primary goal for the NLT translators, not only to facilitate private reading and understanding, but also to ensure that it would be excellent for public reading and make an immediate and powerful impact on any listener.

The Texts behind the New Living Translation
The Old Testament translators used the Masoretic Text of the Hebrew Bible as represented in *Biblia Hebraica Stuttgartensia* (1977), with its extensive system of textual notes; this is an update of Rudolf Kittel's *Biblia Hebraica* (Stuttgart, 1937). The translators also further compared the Dead Sea Scrolls, the Septuagint and other Greek manuscripts, the Samaritan Pentateuch, the Syriac Peshitta, the Latin Vulgate, and any other versions or manuscripts that shed light on the meaning of difficult passages.

The New Testament translators used the two standard editions of the Greek New Testament: the *Greek New Testament*, published by the United Bible Societies (UBS, fourth revised edition, 1993), and *Novum Testamentum Graece*, edited by Nestle and Aland (NA, twenty-seventh edition, 1993). These two editions, which have the same text but differ in punctuation and textual notes, represent, for the most part, the best in modern textual scholarship. However, in cases where strong textual or other scholarly evidence supported the decision, the translators sometimes chose to differ from the UBS and NA Greek texts and followed variant readings found in other ancient witnesses. Significant textual variants of this sort are always noted in the textual notes of the New Living Translation.

Translation Issues
The translators have made a conscious effort to provide a text that can be easily understood by the typical reader of modern English. To this end, we sought to use only vocabulary and

language structures in common use today. We avoided using language likely to become quickly dated or that reflects only a narrow subdialect of English, with the goal of making the New Living Translation as broadly useful and timeless as possible.

But our concern for readability goes beyond the concerns of vocabulary and sentence structure. We are also concerned about historical and cultural barriers to understanding the Bible, and we have sought to translate terms shrouded in history and culture in ways that can be immediately understood. To this end:

- We have converted ancient weights and measures (for example, "ephah" [a unit of dry volume] or "cubit" [a unit of length]) to modern English (American) equivalents, since the ancient measures are not generally meaningful to today's readers. Then in the textual footnotes we offer the literal Hebrew, Aramaic, or Greek measures, along with modern metric equivalents.

- Instead of translating ancient currency values literally, we have expressed them in common terms that communicate the message. For example, in the Old Testament, "ten shekels of silver" becomes "ten pieces of silver" to convey the intended message. In the New Testament, we have often translated the "denarius" as "the normal daily wage" to facilitate understanding. Then a footnote offers: "Greek *a denarius,* the payment for a full day's wage." In general, we give a clear English rendering and then state the literal Hebrew, Aramaic, or Greek in a textual footnote.

- Since the names of Hebrew months are unknown to most contemporary readers, and since the Hebrew lunar calendar fluctuates from year to year in relation to the solar calendar used today, we have looked for clear ways to communicate the time of year the Hebrew months (such as Abib) refer to. When an expanded or interpretive rendering is given in the text, a textual note gives the literal rendering. Where it is possible to define a specific ancient date in terms of our modern calendar, we use modern dates in the text. A textual footnote then gives the literal Hebrew date and states the rationale for our rendering. For example, Ezra 6:15 pinpoints the date when the postexilic Temple was completed in Jerusalem: "the third day of the month Adar." This was during the sixth year of King Darius's reign (that is, 515 B.C.). We have translated that date as March 12, with a footnote giving the Hebrew and identifying the year as 515 B.C.

- Since ancient references to the time of day differ from our modern methods of denoting time, we have used renderings that are instantly understandable to the modern reader. Accordingly, we have rendered specific times of day by using approximate equivalents in terms of our common "o'clock" system. On occasion, translations such as "at dawn the next morning" or "as the sun was setting" have been used when the biblical reference is more general.

- When the meaning of a proper name (or a wordplay inherent in a proper name) is relevant to the message of the text, its meaning is often illuminated with a textual footnote. For example, in Exodus 2:10 the text reads: "The princess named him Moses, for she explained, 'I lifted him out of the water.' " The accompanying footnote reads: "*Moses* sounds like a Hebrew term that means 'to lift out.' "

  Sometimes, when the actual meaning of a name is clear, that meaning is included in parentheses within the text itself. For example, the text at Genesis 16:11 reads: "You are to name him Ishmael *(which means 'God hears'),* for the LORD has heard your cry of distress." Since the original hearers and readers would have instantly understood the meaning of the name "Ishmael," we have provided modern readers with the same information so they can experience the text in a similar way.

- Many words and phrases carry a great deal of cultural meaning that was obvious to the original readers but needs explanation in our own culture. For example, the phrase "they beat their breasts" (Luke 23:48) in ancient times meant that people were very upset, often in mourning. In our translation we chose to translate this phrase dynamically for clarity: "They went home *in deep sorrow.*" Then we included a footnote with the literal Greek, which reads: "Greek *went home beating their breasts.*" In other similar cases, however, we have sometimes chosen to illuminate the existing literal expression to make it immediately understandable. For example, here we might have expanded the literal Greek phrase to read: "They went home beating their breasts *in sorrow.*" If we had done this, we would not have included a textual footnote, since the literal Greek clearly appears in translation.

- Metaphorical language is sometimes difficult for contemporary readers to understand, so at times we have chosen to translate or illuminate the meaning of a metaphor. For example, the ancient poet writes, "Your neck is *like* the tower of David" (Song of Songs 4:4). We have rendered it "Your neck is *as beautiful as* the tower of David" to clarify the intended positive meaning of the simile. Another example comes in Ecclesiastes 12:3, which can be literally rendered: "Remember him . . . when the grinding women cease because they are few, and the women who look through the windows see dimly." We have rendered it: "Remember him before your teeth—your few remaining servants—stop grinding; and before your eyes—the women looking through the windows—see dimly." We clarified such metaphors only when we believed a typical reader might be confused by the literal text.

- When the content of the original language text is poetic in character, we have rendered it in English poetic form. We sought to break lines in ways that clarify and highlight the relationships between phrases of the text. Hebrew poetry often uses parallelism, a literary form where a second phrase (or in some instances a third or fourth) echoes the initial phrase in some way. In Hebrew parallelism, the subsequent parallel phrases continue, while also furthering and sharpening, the thought expressed in the initial line or phrase. Whenever possible, we sought to represent these parallel phrases in natural poetic English.

- The Greek term *hoi Ioudaioi* is literally translated "the Jews" in many English translations. In the Gospel of John, however, this term doesn't always refer to the Jewish people generally. In some contexts, it refers more particularly to the Jewish religious leaders. We have attempted to capture the meaning in these different contexts by using terms such as "the people" (with a footnote: Greek *the Jewish people*) or "the religious leaders," where appropriate.

- One challenge we faced was how to translate accurately the ancient biblical text that was originally written in a context where male-oriented terms were used to refer to humanity generally. We needed to respect the nature of the ancient context while also trying to make the translation clear to a modern audience that tends to read male-oriented language as applying only to males. Often the original text, though using masculine nouns and pronouns, clearly intends that the message be applied to both men and women. A typical example is found in the New Testament letters, where the believers are called "brothers" (*adelphoi*). Yet it is clear from the content of these letters that they were addressed to all the believers—male and female. Thus, we have usually translated this Greek word as "brothers and sisters" in order to represent the historical situation more accurately.

  We have also been sensitive to passages where the text applies generally to human beings or to the human condition. In some instances we have used plural pronouns (they, them) in place of the masculine singular (he, him). For example, a traditional rendering of Proverbs 22:6 is: "Train up a child in the way he should go, and when he is old he will not turn from it." We have rendered it: "Direct your children onto the right path, and when they are older, they will not leave it." At times, we have also replaced third person pronouns with the second person to ensure clarity. A traditional rendering of Proverbs 26:27 is: "He who digs a pit will fall into it, and he who rolls a stone, it will come back on him." We have rendered it: "If you set a trap for others, you will get caught in it yourself. If you roll a boulder down on others, it will crush you instead."

  We should emphasize, however, that all masculine nouns and pronouns used to represent God (for example, "Father") have been maintained without exception. All decisions of this kind have been driven by the concern to reflect accurately the intended meaning of the original texts of Scripture.

Lexical Consistency in Terminology

For the sake of clarity, we have translated certain original-language terms consistently, especially within synoptic passages and for commonly repeated rhetorical phrases, and within certain word categories such as divine names and non-theological technical terminology (e.g., liturgical, legal, cultural, zoological, and botanical terms). For theological terms, we have allowed a greater semantic range of acceptable English words or phrases for a single Hebrew or Greek word. We have avoided some theological terms that are not readily understood by many modern readers. For example, we avoided using words such as "justification" and "sanctification," which are carryovers from Latin translations. In place of these words, we have provided renderings such as "made right with God" and "made holy."

The Spelling of Proper Names

Many individuals in the Bible, especially the Old Testament, are known by more than one name (e.g., Uzziah/Azariah). For the sake of clarity, we have tried to use a single spelling for any one individual, footnoting the literal spelling whenever we differ from it. This is especially helpful in delineating the kings of Israel and Judah. King Joash/Jehoash of Israel has been consistently called Jehoash, while King Joash/Jehoash of Judah is called Joash. A similar distinction has been used to distinguish between Joram/Jehoram of Israel and Joram/Jehoram of Judah. All such decisions were made with the goal of clarifying the text for the reader. When the ancient biblical writers clearly had a theological purpose in their choice of a variant name (e.g., Esh-baal/Ishbosheth), the different names have been maintained with an explanatory footnote.

For the names Jacob and Israel, which are used interchangeably for both the individual patriarch and the nation, we generally render it "Israel" when it refers to the nation and "Jacob" when it refers to the individual. When our rendering of the name differs from the underlying Hebrew text, we provide a textual footnote, which includes this explanation: "The names 'Jacob' and 'Israel' are often interchanged throughout the Old Testament, referring sometimes to the individual patriarch and sometimes to the nation."

The Rendering of Divine Names

All appearances of *'el, 'elohim,* or *'eloah* have been translated "God," except where the context demands the translation "god(s)." We have generally rendered the tetragrammaton (*YHWH*) consistently as "the LORD," utilizing a form with small capitals that is common among English translations. This will distinguish it from the name *'adonai,* which we render "Lord." When *'adonai* and *YHWH* appear together, we have rendered it "Sovereign LORD." This also distinguishes *'adonai YHWH* from cases where *YHWH* appears with *'elohim,* which is rendered "LORD God." When *YH* (the short form of *YHWH*) and *YHWH* appear together, we have rendered it "LORD GOD." When *YHWH* appears with the term *tseba'oth,* we have rendered it "LORD of Heaven's Armies" to translate the meaning of the name. In a few cases, we have utilized the transliteration, *Yahweh,* when the personal character of the name is being invoked in contrast to another divine name or the name of some other god (for example, see Exodus 3:15; 6:2-3).

In the New Testament, the Greek word *christos* has been translated as "Messiah" when the context assumes a Jewish audience. When a Gentile audience can be assumed, *christos* has been translated as "Christ." The Greek word *kurios* is consistently translated "Lord," except that it is translated "LORD" wherever the New Testament text explicitly quotes from the Old Testament, and the text there has it in small capitals.

Textual Footnotes

The New Living Translation provides several kinds of textual footnotes, all designated in the text with an asterisk:

- When for the sake of clarity the NLT renders a difficult or potentially confusing phrase dynamically, we generally give the literal rendering in a textual footnote. This allows the reader to see the literal source of our dynamic rendering and how our translation relates to other more literal translations. These notes are prefaced with "Hebrew," "Aramaic," or "Greek," identifying the language of the underlying source text. For example, in Acts 2:42 we translated the literal "breaking of bread" (from the Greek) as "the Lord's Supper" to clarify that this verse refers to the ceremonial practice of the church rather than just an ordinary meal. Then we attached a footnote to "the Lord's Supper," which reads: "Greek *the breaking of bread.*"

- Textual footnotes are also used to show alternative renderings, prefaced with the word "Or." These normally occur for passages where an aspect of the meaning is debated. On occasion, we also provide notes on words or phrases that represent a departure from long-standing tradition. These notes are prefaced with "Traditionally rendered." For example, the footnote to the translation "serious skin disease" at Leviticus 13:2 says: "Traditionally rendered *leprosy*. The Hebrew word used throughout this passage is used to describe various skin diseases."

- When our translators follow a textual variant that differs significantly from our standard Hebrew or Greek texts (listed earlier), we document that difference with a footnote. We also footnote cases when the NLT excludes a passage that is included in the Greek text known as the *Textus Receptus* (and familiar to readers through its translation in the King James Version). In such cases, we offer a translation of the excluded text in a footnote, even though it is generally recognized as a later addition to the Greek text and not part of the original Greek New Testament.

- All Old Testament passages that are quoted in the New Testament are identified by a textual footnote at the New Testament location. When the New Testament clearly quotes from the Greek translation of the Old Testament, and when it differs significantly in wording from the Hebrew text, we also place a textual footnote at the Old Testament location. This note includes a rendering of the Greek version, along with a cross-reference to the New Testament passage(s) where it is cited (for example, see notes on Psalms 8:2; 53:3; Proverbs 3:12).

- Some textual footnotes provide cultural and historical information on places, things, and people in the Bible that are probably obscure to modern readers. Such notes should aid the reader in understanding the message of the text. For example, in Acts 12:1, "King Herod" is named in this translation as "King Herod Agrippa" and is identified in a footnote as being "the nephew of Herod Antipas and a grandson of Herod the Great."

- When the meaning of a proper name (or a wordplay inherent in a proper name) is relevant to the meaning of the text, it is either illuminated with a textual footnote or included within parentheses in the text itself. For example, the footnote concerning the name "Eve" at Genesis 3:20 reads: "*Eve* sounds like a Hebrew term that means 'to give life.'" This wordplay in the Hebrew illuminates the meaning of the text, which goes on to say that Eve "would be the mother of all who live."

AS WE SUBMIT this translation for publication, we recognize that any translation of the Scriptures is subject to limitations and imperfections. Anyone who has attempted to communicate the richness of God's Word into another language will realize it is impossible to make a perfect translation. Recognizing these limitations, we sought God's guidance and wisdom throughout this project. Now we pray that he will accept our efforts and use this translation for the benefit of the church and of all people.

We pray that the New Living Translation will overcome some of the barriers of history, culture, and language that have kept people from reading and understanding God's Word. We hope that readers unfamiliar with the Bible will find the words clear and easy to understand and that readers well versed in the Scriptures will gain a fresh perspective. We pray that readers will gain insight and wisdom for living, but most of all that they will meet the God of the Bible and be forever changed by knowing him.

The Bible Translation Committee
October 2007

WHY THE
LIFE APPLICATION STUDY BIBLE
IS UNIQUE

Have you ever opened your Bible and asked the following:

- What does this passage really mean?
- How does it apply to my life?
- Why does some of the Bible seem irrelevant?
- What do these ancient cultures have to do with today?
- I love God; why can't I understand what he is saying to me through his word?
- What's going on in the lives of these Bible people?

Many Christians do not read the Bible regularly. Why? Because in the pressures of daily living they cannot find a connection between the timeless principles of Scripture and the ever-present problems of day-by-day living.

God urges us to apply his word (Isaiah 42:23; 1 Corinthians 10:11; 2 Thessalonians 3:4), but too often we stop at accumulating Bible knowledge. This is why the *Life Application Study Bible* was developed—to show how to put into practice what we have learned.

Applying God's word is a vital part of one's relationship with God; it is the evidence that we are obeying him. The difficulty in applying the Bible is not with the Bible itself, but with the reader's inability to bridge the gap between the past and present, the conceptual and practical. When we don't or can't do this, spiritual dryness, shallowness, and indifference are the results.

The words of Scripture itself cry out to us, "But don't just listen to God's word. You must do what it says. Otherwise, you are only fooling yourselves" (James 1:22). The *Life Application Study Bible* helps us to obey God's word. Developed by an interdenominational team of pastors, scholars, family counselors, and a national organization dedicated to promoting God's word and spreading the gospel, the *Life Application Study Bible* took many years to complete. All the work was reviewed by several renowned theologians under the directorship of Dr. Kenneth Kantzer.

The *Life Application Study Bible* does what a good resource Bible should: It helps you understand the context of a passage, gives important background and historical information, explains difficult words and phrases, and helps you see the interrelationship of Scripture. But it does much more. The *Life Application Study Bible* goes deeper into God's word, helping you discover the timeless truth being communicated, see the relevance for your life, and make a personal application. While some study Bibles attempt application, over 75 percent of this Bible is application oriented. The notes answer the questions "So what?" and "What does this passage mean to me, my family, my friends, my job, my neighborhood, my church, my country?"

Imagine reading a familiar passage of Scripture and gaining fresh insight, as if it were the first time you had ever read it. How much richer your life would be if you left each Bible reading with a new perspective and a small change for the better. A small change every day adds up to a changed life—and that is the very purpose of Scripture.

WHAT IS APPLICATION?

The best way to define application is to first determine what it is *not*. Application is *not* just accumulating knowledge. Accumulating knowledge helps us discover and understand facts and concepts, but it stops there. History is filled with philosophers who knew what the Bible said but failed to apply it to their lives, keeping them from believing and changing. Many think that understanding is the end goal of Bible study, but it is really only the beginning.

Application is *not* just illustration. Illustration only tells us how someone else handled a similar situation. While we may empathize with that person, we still have little direction for our personal situation.

Application is *not* just making a passage "relevant." Making the Bible relevant only helps us to see that the same lessons that were true in Bible times are true today; it does not show us how to apply them to the problems and pressures of our individual lives.

What, then, is application? Application begins by knowing and understanding God's word and its timeless truths. *But you cannot stop there*. If you do, God's word may not change your life, and it may become dull, difficult, tedious, and tiring. A good application focuses the truth of God's word, shows the reader what to do about what is being read, and motivates the reader to respond to what God is teaching. All three are essential to application.

Application is putting into practice what we already know (see Mark 4:24 and Hebrews 5:14) and answering the question "So what?" by confronting us with the right questions and motivating us to take action (see 1 John 2:5-6 and James 2:26). Application is deeply personal—unique for each individual. It makes a relevant truth a personal truth and involves developing a strategy and action plan to live your life in harmony with the Bible. It is the biblical "how to" of life.

You may ask, "How can your application notes be relevant to my life?" Each application note has three parts: (1) an *explanation*, which ties the note directly to the Scripture passage and sets up the truth that is being taught; (2) the *bridge*, which explains the timeless truth and makes it relevant for today; (3) the *application*, which shows you how to take the timeless truth and apply it to your personal situation. No note, by itself, can apply Scripture directly to your life. It can only teach, direct, lead, guide, inspire, recommend, and urge. It can give you the resources and direction you need to apply the Bible, but only you can take these resources and put them into practice.

A good note, therefore, should not only give you knowledge and understanding but point you to application. Before you buy any kind of resource study Bible, you should evaluate the notes and ask the following questions: (1) Does the note contain enough information to help me understand the point of the Scripture passage? (2) Does the note assume I know more than I do? (3) Does the note avoid denominational bias? (4) Do the notes touch most of life's experiences? (5) Does the note help me apply God's word?

FEATURES OF THE
LIFE APPLICATION STUDY BIBLE

NOTES
In addition to providing the reader with many application notes, the *Life Application Study Bible* also offers several kinds of explanatory notes, which help the reader understand culture, history, context, difficult-to-understand passages, background, places, theological concepts, and the relationship of various passages in Scripture to other passages.

BOOK INTRODUCTIONS
Each book introduction is divided into several easy-to-find parts:

Timeline. A guide that puts the Bible book into its historical setting. It lists the key events and the dates when they occurred.

Vital Statistics. A list of straight facts about the book—those pieces of information you need to know at a glance.

Overview. A summary of the book with general lessons and applications that can be learned from the book as a whole.

Blueprint. The outline of the book. It is printed in easy-to-understand language and is designed for easy memorization. To the right of each main heading is a key lesson that is taught in that particular section.

Megathemes. A section that gives the main themes of the Bible book, explains their significance, and then tells you why they are still important for us today.

Map. If included, this shows the key places found in that book and retells the story of the book from a geographical point of view.

OUTLINE
The *Life Application Study Bible* has a new, custom-made outline that was designed specifically from an application point of view. Several unique features should be noted:

1. To avoid confusion and to aid memory work, the book outline has only three levels for headings. Main outline heads are marked with a capital letter. Subheads are marked by a number. Minor explanatory heads have no letter or number.

2. Each main outline head marked by a letter also has a brief paragraph below it summarizing the Bible text and offering a general application.

3. Parallel passages are listed where they apply.

PERSONALITY PROFILES
Among the unique features of this Bible are the profiles of key Bible people, including their strengths and weaknesses, greatest accomplishments and mistakes, and key lessons from their lives.

MAPS

The *Life Application Study Bible* has a thorough and comprehensive Bible atlas built right into the book. There are two kinds of maps: a book-introduction map, telling the story of the book, and thumbnail maps in the notes, plotting most geographic movements.

CHARTS AND DIAGRAMS

Many charts and diagrams are included to help the reader better visualize difficult concepts or relationships. Most charts not only present the needed information but show the significance of the information as well.

CROSS-REFERENCES

An updated, exhaustive cross-reference system in the margins of the Bible text helps the reader find related passages quickly.

TEXTUAL NOTES

Directly related to the text of the New Living Translation, the textual notes provide explanations on certain wording in the translation, alternate translations, and information about readings in the ancient manuscripts.

HIGHLIGHTED NOTES

In each Bible study lesson, you will be asked to read specific notes as part of your preparation. These notes have each been highlighted by a bullet (•) so that you can find them easily.

1 & 2 TIMOTHY

1 TIMOTHY

VITAL STATISTICS

PURPOSE:
To give encouragement and instruction to Timothy, a young leader

AUTHOR:
Paul

ORIGINAL AUDIENCE:
Timothy, Paul's son in the faith

DATE WRITTEN:
Approximately A.D. 64, from Rome or Macedonia (possibly Philippi), probably just prior to Paul's final imprisonment in Rome

SETTING:
Timothy was one of Paul's closest companions. Paul had sent Timothy to the church at Ephesus to counter the false teaching that had arisen there (1:3, 4). Timothy probably served for a time as a leader in the church at Ephesus. Paul hoped to visit Timothy (3:14, 15; 4:13), but in the meantime, he wrote this letter to give Timothy practical advice about the ministry.

KEY VERSE:
"Don't let anyone think less of you because you are young. Be an example to all believers in what you say, in the way you live, in your love, your faith, and your purity" (4:12).

KEY PEOPLE:
Paul, Timothy

KEY PLACE:
Ephesus

SPECIAL FEATURES:
First Timothy is a personal letter and a handbook of church administration and discipline.

WITHOUT trying, we model our values. Parents in particular demonstrate to their children what they consider important and valuable. "Like father, like son" is not just a well-worn cliché; it is a truth repeated in our homes. And experience proves that children often follow the life-styles of their parents, repeating their successes and mistakes.

Timothy is a prime example of one who was influenced by godly relatives. His mother, Eunice, and grandmother, Lois, were Jewish believers who helped shape his life and promote his spiritual growth (2 Timothy 1:5; 3:15). The first "second generation" Christian mentioned in the New Testament, Timothy became Paul's protégé and pastor of the church at Ephesus. As a young minister, Timothy faced all sorts of pressures, conflicts, and challenges from the church and his surrounding culture. To counsel and encourage Timothy, Paul sent this very personal letter.

Paul wrote 1 Timothy in about A.D. 64, probably just prior to his final Roman imprisonment. Because he had appealed to Caesar, Paul had been sent as a prisoner to Rome (see Acts 25—28). Most scholars believe that Paul was released about A.D. 62 (possibly because the "statute of limitations" had expired), and that during the next few years he was able to travel. During this time, he wrote 1 Timothy and Titus. Soon, however, Emperor Nero began his campaign to eliminate Christianity. It is believed that during this time Paul was imprisoned again and eventually executed. During this second Roman imprisonment, Paul wrote 2 Timothy. Titus and the two letters to Timothy comprise what are called the "Pastoral Letters."

Paul's first letter to Timothy affirms their relationship (1:2). Paul begins his fatherly advice, warning Timothy about false teachers (1:3–11) and urging him to hold on to his faith in Christ (1:12–20). Next, Paul considers public worship, emphasizing the importance of prayer (2:1–7) and order in church meetings (2:8–15). This leads to a discussion of the qualifications of church leaders—elders and deacons. Here Paul lists specific criteria for each office (3:1–16).

Paul speaks again about false teachers, telling Timothy how to recognize them and respond to them (4:1–16). Next, he gives practical advice on pastoral care to the young and old (5:1, 2), widows (5:3–16), elders (5:17–25), and slaves (6:1, 2). Paul concludes by exhorting Timothy to guard his motives (6:3–10), to stand firm in his faith (6:11, 12), to live above reproach (6:13–16), and to minister faithfully (6:17–21).

First Timothy holds many lessons. If you are a church leader, take note of Paul's relationship with this young disciple—his careful counsel and guidance. Measure yourself against the qualifications that Paul gives for elders and deacons. If you are young in the faith, follow the example of godly Christian leaders like Timothy, who imitated Paul's life. If you are a parent, remind yourself of the profound effect a Christian home can have on family members. A faithful mother and grandmother led Timothy to Christ, and Timothy's ministry helped change the world.

THE BLUEPRINT

1. Instructions on right belief
   (1:1–20)
2. Instructions for the church
   (2:1—3:16)
3. Instructions for elders
   (4:1—6:21)

Paul advised Timothy on such practical topics as qualifications for church leaders, public worship, confronting false teaching, and how to treat various groups of people within the church. Right belief and right behavior are critical for anyone who desires to lead or serve effectively in the church. We should all believe rightly, participate in church actively, and minister to one another lovingly.

MEGATHEMES

THEME	EXPLANATION	IMPORTANCE
Sound Doctrine	Paul instructed Timothy to preserve the Christian faith by teaching sound doctrine and modeling right living. Timothy had to oppose false teachers, who were leading church members away from belief in salvation by faith in Jesus Christ alone.	We must know the truth in order to defend it. We must cling to the belief that Christ came to save us. We should stay away from those who twist the words of the Bible for their own purposes.
Public Worship	Prayer in public worship must be done with a proper attitude toward God and fellow believers.	Christian character must be evident in every aspect of worship. We must rid ourselves of any anger, resentment, or offensive behavior that might disrupt worship or damage church unity.
Church Leadership	Paul gives specific instructions concerning the qualifications for church leaders so that the church might honor God and operate smoothly.	Church leaders must be wholly committed to Christ. If you are a new or young Christian, don't be anxious to become a leader in the church. Seek to develop your Christian character first. Be sure to seek God, not your own ambition.
Personal Discipline	It takes discipline to be a leader in the church. Timothy, like all pastors, had to guard his motives, minister faithfully, and live above reproach. Any pastor must keep morally and spiritually fit.	To stay in good spiritual shape, you must discipline yourself to study God's Word and to obey it. Put your spiritual abilities to work!
Caring Church	The church has a responsibility to care for the needs of all its members, especially the sick, the poor, and the widowed. Caring must go beyond good intentions.	Caring for the family of believers demonstrates our Christlike attitude and exhibits genuine love to non-believers.

1. Instructions on right belief

Greetings from Paul

1:1
Col 1:27
Titus 1:3; 3:4

1:2
Acts 16:1
2 Tim 1:2
Titus 1:4

1 This letter is from Paul, an apostle of Christ Jesus, appointed by the command of God our Savior and Christ Jesus, who gives us hope. ²I am writing to Timothy, my true son in the faith.

May God the Father and Christ Jesus our Lord give you grace, mercy, and peace.

• **1:1** This letter was written to Timothy in A.D. 64 or 65, after Paul's first imprisonment in Rome (Acts 28:16-31). Apparently Paul had been out of prison for several years, and during that time he had revisited many churches in Asia and Macedonia. When he and Timothy returned to Ephesus, they found widespread false teaching in the church. Paul had warned the Ephesian elders to be on guard against the false teachers who inevitably would come after he had left (Acts 20:17-31). Paul sent Timothy to lead the Ephesian church while he moved on to Macedonia. From there Paul wrote this letter of encouragement and instruction to help Timothy deal with the difficult situation in the Ephesian church.

Later, Paul was arrested again and brought back to a Roman prison.

1:1 Paul calls himself an *apostle*, meaning "one who is sent." Paul was sent by Jesus Christ to bring the message of salvation to the Gentiles (Acts 9:1-20). He was an apostle "by the command of God" because in Acts 13:2, the Holy Spirit, through the prophets, said, "Dedicate Barnabas and Saul [Paul] for the special work to which I have called them." From Romans 16:25, 26 and Titus 1:3, it is obvious that Paul regarded his commission as direct from God. For more information on Paul, see his Profile in Acts 9, p. 1837.

Warnings against False Teachings

3 When I left for Macedonia, I urged you to stay there in Ephesus and stop those whose teaching is contrary to the truth. 4 Don't let them waste their time in endless discussion of myths and spiritual pedigrees. These things only lead to meaningless speculations,* which don't help people live a life of faith in God.*

5 The purpose of my instruction is that all believers would be filled with love that comes from a pure heart, a clear conscience, and genuine faith. 6 But some people have missed this whole point. They have turned away from these things and spend their time in meaningless discussions. 7 They want to be known as teachers of the law of Moses, but they don't know what they are talking about, even though they speak so confidently.

8 We know that the law is good when used correctly. 9 For the law was not intended for people who do what is right. It is for people who are lawless and rebellious, who are ungodly and sinful, who consider nothing sacred and defile what is holy, who kill their father or mother or commit other murders. 10 The law is for people who are sexually immoral, or who practice homosexuality, or are slave traders,* liars, promise breakers, or who do anything else that contradicts the wholesome teaching 11 that comes from the glorious Good News entrusted to me by our blessed God.

Paul's Gratitude for God's Mercy

12 I thank Christ Jesus our Lord, who has given me strength to do his work. He considered me trustworthy and appointed me to serve him, 13 even though I used to blaspheme the name of Christ. In my insolence, I persecuted his people. But God had mercy on me because I did it in ignorance and unbelief. 14 Oh, how generous and gracious our Lord was! He filled me with the faith and love that come from Christ Jesus.

1:4a Greek *in myths and endless genealogies, which cause speculation.* **1:4b** Greek *a stewardship of God in faith.* **1:10** Or *kidnappers.*

1:3
Acts 20:1
Gal 1:6-7
1 Tim 6:3

1:4
1 Tim 4:7
Titus 3:9

1:5
Rom 13:10
Gal 5:14
2 Tim 1:5

1:6
2 Tim 2:23
Titus 1:10

1:9
Gal 3:19; 5:23

1:10
1 Tim 6:3
2 Tim 4:3
Titus 1:9; 2:1

1:11
Gal 2:7

1:12
Acts 9:15
Gal 1:15-16
Phil 4:13

1:13
Acts 8:3; 26:9
1 Cor 15:9

1:14
Rom 5:20
2 Tim 1:13

1:3, 4 Paul first visited Ephesus on his second missionary journey (Acts 18:19-21). Later, on his third missionary journey, he stayed there for almost three years (Acts 19–20). Ephesus, along with Rome, Corinth, Antioch, and Alexandria, was one of the major cities in the Roman Empire. It was a center for the commerce, politics, and religions of Asia Minor, and the location of the temple dedicated to the goddess Artemis (Diana).

• **1:3, 4** The church at Ephesus may have been plagued by the same heresy that was threatening the church at Colosse—the teaching that to be acceptable to God, a person had to discover certain hidden knowledge and had to worship angels (Colossians 2:8, 18). The false teachers were motivated by their own interests rather than Christ's. They embroiled the church in endless and irrelevant questions and controversies, taking precious time away from the study of the truth. Stay away from religious speculation and pointless theological arguments. Such exercises may seem harmless at first, but they have a way of sidetracking us from the central message of the Good News—the person and work of Jesus Christ. They expend time we should use to share the Good News with others, and they don't help people grow in the faith. Avoid anything that keeps you from doing God's work.

• **1:3-7** Many leaders and authorities today demand allegiance, some of whom would even have us turn from Christ to follow them. When they seem to know the Bible, their influence can be dangerously subtle. They are modern-day false teachers. How can you recognize false teachers? (1) They teach what is contrary to the truth found in Scripture (1:3; 1:6, 7; 4:1-3). (2) They promote trivial and divisive controversies instead of helping people come to Jesus (1:4). (3) They aren't concerned about personal evidence of God's presence in their lives, spending their time on "meaningless discussions" instead (1:6). (4) Their motivation is to make a name for themselves (1:7). To protect yourself from the deception of false teachers, learn what the Bible teaches and remain steadfast in your faith in Christ alone.

• **1:6** Arguing about details of the Bible can send us off on interesting but irrelevant tangents and cause us to miss the intent of God's message. The false teachers at Ephesus constructed vast speculative systems and then argued about the minor details of their wholly imaginary ideas. We should allow nothing to distract us from the Good News of salvation in Jesus Christ, the main point of Scripture. We should know what the Bible says, apply it to our lives daily, and teach it to others. When we do this, we will be able to evaluate all teachings in light of the central truth about Jesus.

1:7-11 The false teachers wanted to become famous as teachers of God's law, but they didn't even understand the law's purpose. The law was not meant to give believers a list of commands for every occasion but to show unbelievers their sin and bring them to God. For more of what Paul taught about our relationship to law, see Romans 5:20, 21; 13:9, 10; Galatians 3:24-29.

1:10 Some attempt to legitimize homosexuality as an acceptable alternative lifestyle. Even some Christians say people have a right to choose their sexual preference. But the entire Bible (both in the Old and New Testaments) calls homosexual behavior sin (see Leviticus 18:22; Romans 1:18-32; 1 Corinthians 6:9-11). We must be careful, however, to condemn only the practice and not the people. People who live this lifestyle can be forgiven, and their lives can be transformed. The church should be a haven of forgiveness and healing for repentant homosexuals without compromising its stance against homosexual behavior. For more on this subject see the notes on Romans 1:26, 27.

1:12-17 People can feel so guilt-ridden by their past that they think God could never forgive and accept them. But consider Paul's past. He had scoffed at the teachings of Jesus and had hunted down and murdered God's people before coming to faith in Christ (Acts 9:1-9). God forgave Paul and used him mightily for his Kingdom. No matter how shameful your past, God also can forgive and use you.

1:14 Paul's boldness in Christ can be intimidating. We may feel that our faith in God and our love for Christ and for others will always be inadequate. We will experience times of failure. But we can remain confident that Christ will help our faith and love grow as our relationship with him deepens. Paul's prayer for the Philippians applies to us also: "I am certain that God, who began the good work within you, will continue his work until it is finally finished on the day when Christ Jesus returns" (Philippians 1:6).

1:15
Luke 15:2; 19:10
Rom 5:8

¹⁵This is a trustworthy saying, and everyone should accept it: "Christ Jesus came into the world to save sinners"—and I am the worst of them all. ¹⁶But God had mercy on me so that Christ Jesus could use me as a prime example of his great patience with even the worst sinners. Then others will realize that they, too, can believe in him and receive eternal life. ¹⁷All

1:17
Rom 16:27
1 Tim 6:15

honor and glory to God forever and ever! He is the eternal King, the unseen one who never dies; he alone is God. Amen.

Timothy's Responsibility

1:18
1 Tim 6:12
1:19
2 Tim 4:7
1:20
1 Cor 5:5
2 Tim 2:17; 4:14

¹⁸Timothy, my son, here are my instructions for you, based on the prophetic words spoken about you earlier. May they help you fight well in the Lord's battles. ¹⁹Cling to your faith in Christ, and keep your conscience clear. For some people have deliberately violated their consciences; as a result, their faith has been shipwrecked. ²⁰Hymenaeus and Alexander are two examples. I threw them out and handed them over to Satan so they might learn not to blaspheme God.

2. Instructions for the church

Instructions about Worship

2:2
Rom 13:1
2:4
1 Tim 4:10
2 Tim 2:25

2 I urge you, first of all, to pray for all people. Ask God to help them; intercede on their behalf, and give thanks for them. ²Pray this way for kings and all who are in authority so that we can live peaceful and quiet lives marked by godliness and dignity. ³This is good and pleases God our Savior, ⁴who wants everyone to be saved and to understand the truth.

1:15 Here Paul summarizes the Good News: Jesus came into the world to save sinners, and no sinner is beyond his saving power. (See Luke 5:32 for Jesus' purpose for being on earth.) Jesus didn't come merely to show us how to live better lives or to challenge us to be better people. He came to offer us salvation that leads to eternal life. Have you accepted his offer?

1:15 Paul was not nearly as interested in creating an image as he was in being an example. He did not hesitate to share his past, because he knew his failures would allow others to have hope. At times we hesitate to share our past struggles with others because we are afraid it will tarnish our image. Paul demonstrated that lowering our guard can be an important step in communicating the gospel. People will not believe the gospel is important if they can't see that it is crucial in your life. How has Christ shown patience with you? Did he stay with you when you doubted and rebelled? Did he remain faithful when you ignored his prior claim on your life? Did he love you when you disregarded his Word and his church? Remember that his patience is unlimited for those who love him. Don't be afraid to let others know what Christ has done for you.

1:18 Paul highly valued the gift of prophecy (1 Corinthians 14:1). Through prophecy important messages of warning and encouragement came to the church. Just as pastors are ordained and set apart for ministry in church today, Timothy had been set apart for ministry when elders laid their hands on him (see 4:14). Apparently at this ceremony, several believers had prophesied about Timothy's gifts and strengths. These words from the Lord must have encouraged Timothy throughout his ministry.

• **1:19** How can you keep your conscience clear? Treasure your faith in Christ more than anything else and do what you know is right. Each time you deliberately ignore your conscience, you are hardening your heart. Over a period of time your capacity to tell right from wrong will diminish. As you walk with God, he will speak to you through your conscience, letting you know the difference between right and wrong. Be sure to act on those inner tugs so that you do what is right—then your conscience will remain clear.

1:20 We don't know who Alexander was—he may have been an associate of Hymenaeus. Hymenaeus's error is explained in 2 Timothy 2:17, 18. He weakened people's faith by teaching that the resurrection had already occurred. Paul says that he handed both of these men over to Satan, meaning that Paul had removed them from the fellowship of the church. Paul did this so that they would see their error and repent. The ultimate purpose of this

punishment was correction. The church today is too often lax in disciplining Christians who deliberately sin. Deliberate disobedience should be responded to quickly and sternly to prevent the entire congregation from being affected. But discipline must be done in a way that tries to bring the offender back to Christ and into the loving embrace of the church. The definition of discipline includes these words: strengthening, purifying, training, correcting, perfecting. Condemnation, suspicion, withholding of forgiveness, or permanent exile should not be a part of church discipline.

• **2:1-4** Although God is all-powerful and all-knowing, he has chosen to let us help him change the world through our prayers. How this works is a mystery to us because of our limited understanding, but it is a reality. Paul based his instruction about prayer for *everyone* on his conviction that God's invitation for salvation extends equally to all people. The word *everyone* captures the nature of the gospel. The world that God loves includes every person (John 3:16). He loves us as individuals whom he knows intimately (Psalm 139:13-18). Paul urges us to pray for "all people." Our earnest prayers will have powerful results (James 5:16).

• **2:2** We should pray for those in authority around the world so that their societies will be conducive to the spread of the Good News. Paul's command to pray for kings is remarkable considering that Nero, a notoriously cruel ruler, was emperor at this time (A.D. 54–68). When Paul wrote this letter, persecution was a growing threat to believers. Later, when Nero needed a scapegoat for the great fire that destroyed much of Rome in A.D. 64, he blamed the Roman Christians so as to take the focus off himself. Then persecution erupted throughout the Roman Empire. Not only were Christians denied certain privileges in society, some were even publicly butchered, burned, or fed to animals.

2:4 Both Peter and Paul said that God wants everyone to be saved (see 2 Peter 3:9). This does not mean that all *will* be saved, because the Bible makes it clear that many reject Christ (Matthew 25:31-46; John 12:44-50; Hebrews 10:26-29). The Good News has a universal scope; it is not directed only to people of one race, one sex, or one national background. God loves the whole world and sent his Son to save sinners. No one is outside God's mercy or beyond the reach of his offer of salvation.

⁵For there is only one God and one Mediator who can reconcile God and humanity—the man Christ Jesus. ⁶He gave his life to purchase freedom for everyone. This is the message God gave to the world at just the right time. ⁷And I have been chosen as a preacher and apostle to teach the Gentiles this message about faith and truth. I'm not exaggerating—just telling the truth.

⁸In every place of worship, I want men to pray with holy hands lifted up to God, free from anger and controversy.

⁹And I want women to be modest in their appearance.* They should wear decent and appropriate clothing and not draw attention to themselves by the way they fix their hair or by wearing gold or pearls or expensive clothes. ¹⁰For women who claim to be devoted to God should make themselves attractive by the good things they do.

¹¹Women should learn quietly and submissively. ¹²I do not let women teach men or have authority over them.* Let them listen quietly. ¹³For God made Adam first, and afterward he made Eve. ¹⁴And it was not Adam who was deceived by Satan. The woman was deceived, and sin was the result. ¹⁵But women will be saved through childbearing,* assuming they continue to live in faith, love, holiness, and modesty.

2:9 Or *to pray in modest apparel.*   **2:12** Or *teach men or usurp their authority.*   **2:15** Or *will be saved by accepting their role as mothers,* or *will be saved by the birth of the Child.*

2:5
Rom 3:29-30
2:6
Gal 1:4; 2:20
2:7
Acts 9:15
2 Tim 1:1
2:8
Pss 24:4; 63:4
2:9
1 Pet 3:3-5
2:11
1 Cor 14:34
2:12
Eph 5:22
2:13
Gen 1:27; 2:7, 22
2:14
Gen 3:1-6, 13

2:5, 6 Though some people think there are many ways to God, in practice, each person must choose a single way. We can stand on one side of a gorge and discuss the possibility of many bridges across the abyss, but if we are determined to cross, we will have to commit to one bridge. Those who insist that there are many bridges to God usually fit one of the following categories: (1) They have not personally committed to any "bridge." They are surprised that their belief in multiple ways does not exempt them from having to choose one. (2) Their belief in "many ways to God" hides their true belief that finding God doesn't really matter at all. (3) They are convinced that arguing for "many ways to God" will insure that they won't be wrong. If there is only one way, their generalized belief will presumably have included it. (4) They have decided that believing in "many ways to God" requires less work than going to the trouble of actually considering the claims of various religious systems.

The facts remain: We human beings are separated from God by sin and we need a Savior—a way across the abyss of sin and back to God. Only one person in the universe is our Mediator and can stand between us and God and bring us together again—Jesus, who is both God and man. Jesus' sacrifice brought new life to all people. Have you let him bridge the gap between you and God?

2:7 Paul describes himself as a preacher and apostle. He was given the special privilege of announcing the Good News to the Gentiles. He gives his credentials as an apostle in 1 Corinthians 15:7-11.

• **2:8** Besides displeasing God, anger and controversy make prayer difficult. That is why Jesus said that we should interrupt our prayers, if necessary, to make peace with others (Matthew 5:23, 24). God wants us to obey him immediately and thoroughly. Our goal should be to have a right relationship with God and also with others.

2:9, 10 It is not unscriptural for a woman to want to be attractive. Today, however, to what degree should women take this advice about fixing their hair or wearing gold, pearls, or expensive clothes? Paul was not prohibiting these things; he was simply saying that women should not be drawing attention to themselves through these things. Modesty and decency are the key words. All women would do well to remember that beauty begins on the inside. A gentle, modest, loving character gives a light to the face that cannot be duplicated by even the best cosmetics. A carefully groomed and well-decorated exterior is artificial and cold unless inner beauty is present. The general rule for both women and men emphasizes that both behavior and dress must express submission to and respect for Jesus Christ.

2:9-15 To understand these verses, we must understand the situation in which Paul and Timothy worked. In first-century Jewish culture, women were not allowed to study. When Paul said that

women should "learn quietly and submissively," he was offering them an amazing new opportunity to learn God's Word. That they were to listen and learn quietly and submissively referred to an attitude of quietness and composure (not total silence). In addition, Paul himself acknowledges that women publicly prayed and prophesied (1 Corinthians 11:5). Apparently, however, the women in the Ephesian church were abusing their newly acquired Christian freedom. Because these women were new converts, they did not yet have the necessary experience, knowledge, or Christian maturity to teach those who already had extensive scriptural education.

2:12 Some interpret this passage to mean that women should never teach in the assembled church; however, commentators point out that Paul did not forbid women from ever teaching. Paul's commended co-worker, Priscilla, taught Apollos, the great preacher (Acts 18:24-26). Paul frequently mentioned other women who held positions of responsibility in the church. Phoebe worked in the church (Romans 16:1). Mary, Tryphena, Tryphosa and Persis were the Lord's workers (Romans 16:6, 12), as were Euodia and Syntyche (Philippians 4:2). Paul was very likely prohibiting the Ephesian women, not all women, from teaching (see the note on 2:9-15).

Paul did not want the Ephesian women to teach because they didn't yet have enough knowledge or experience. The Ephesian church had a particular problem with false teachers. Evidently the women were especially susceptible to the false teachings (2 Timothy 3:1-9) because they did not yet have enough biblical knowledge to discern the truth. In addition, some of the women were apparently flaunting their newfound Christian freedom by wearing inappropriate clothing (2:9). Paul was telling Timothy not to put anyone (in this case, women) into a position of leadership who was not yet mature in the faith (see 3:6; 5:22). The same principle applies to churches today (see the note on 3:6).

2:13, 14 In previous letters Paul had discussed male/female roles in marriage (Ephesians 5:21-33; Colossians 3:18, 19). Here he talks about male/female roles within the church. Some scholars see these verses about Adam and Eve as an illustration of what was happening in the Ephesian church. Just as Eve had been deceived in the Garden of Eden, so the women in the church were being deceived by false teachers. And just as Adam was the first human created by God, so the men in the church in Ephesus should be the first to speak and teach, because they had more training. This view, then, stresses that Paul's teaching here is not universal but applies to churches with similar problems. Other scholars, however, contend that the roles Paul points out are God's design for his created order—God established these roles to maintain harmony in both the family and the church.

2:14 Paul is not excusing Adam for his part in the Fall (Genesis 3:6, 7, 17-19). On the contrary, in his letter to the Romans Paul

TIMOTHY

Painful lessons are usually doorways to new opportunities. Even the apostle Paul had much to learn. Shortly after his disappointing experience with John Mark, Paul recruited another eager young man, Timothy, to be his assistant. Paul's intense personality may have been too much for John Mark to handle. It could easily have created the same problem for Timothy. But Paul seems to have learned a lesson in patience from his old friend Barnabas. As a result, Timothy became a "son" to Paul.

Timothy probably became a Christian after Paul's first missionary visit to Lystra (Acts 16:1-5). Timothy already had solid Jewish training in the Scriptures from his mother and grandmother. By Paul's second visit, Timothy had grown into a respected disciple of Jesus. He did not hesitate to join Paul and Silas on their journey. His willingness to be circumcised as an adult is clearly a mark of his commitment. (Timothy's mixed Greek/Jewish background could have created problems on their missionary journeys, because many of their audiences would be made up of Jews who were concerned about the strict keeping of this tradition. Timothy's submission to the rite of circumcision helped to avoid that potential problem.)

Beyond the tensions created by his mixed racial background, Timothy seemed to struggle with a naturally timid character and a sensitivity to his youthfulness. Unfortunately, many who share Timothy's character traits are quickly written off as too great a risk to deserve much responsibility. By God's grace, Paul saw great potential in Timothy. Paul demonstrated his confidence in Timothy by entrusting him with important responsibilities. Paul sent Timothy as his personal representative to Corinth during a particularly tense time (1 Corinthians 4:14-17). Although Timothy was apparently ineffective in that difficult mission, Paul did not give up on him. Timothy continued to travel with Paul.

Our last pictures of Timothy come from the most personal letters in the New Testament: 1 and 2 Timothy. The aging apostle Paul was near the end of his life, but his burning desire to continue his mission had not dimmed. Paul was writing to one of his closest friends—they had traveled, suffered, cried, and laughed together. They shared the intense joy of seeing people respond to the Good News and the agonies of seeing the gospel rejected and distorted. Paul left Timothy in Ephesus to oversee the young church there (1 Timothy 1:3-4). He wrote to encourage Timothy and give him needed direction. These letters have provided comfort and help to countless other "Timothys" through the years. When you face a challenge that seems beyond your abilities, read 1 and 2 Timothy, and remember that others have shared your experience.

Strengths and accomplishments	• Became a believer during Paul's first missionary journey and joined him for his other two journeys • Was a respected Christian in his hometown • Was Paul's special representative on several occasions • Received two personal letters from Paul • Probably knew Paul better than any other person, becoming like a son to Paul
Weaknesses and mistakes	• Struggled with a timid and reserved nature • Allowed others to look down on his youthfulness • Was apparently unable to correct some of the problems in the church at Corinth when Paul sent him there
Lessons from his life	• Youthfulness should not be an excuse for ineffectiveness • Our inadequacies and inabilities should not keep us from being available to God
Vital statistics	• Where: Lystra • Occupations: Missionary, pastor • Relatives: Mother: Eunice. Grandmother: Lois. Father: a Greek. • Contemporaries: Paul, Silas, Luke, Mark, Peter, Barnabas
Key verses	"I have no one else like Timothy, who genuinely cares about your welfare. All the others care only for themselves and not for what matters to Jesus Christ. But you know how Timothy has proved himself. Like a son with his father, he has served with me in preaching the Good News" (Philippians 2:20-22).

Timothy's story is told in Acts, starting in chapter 16. He is also mentioned in Romans 16:21; 1 Corinthians 4:17; 16:10-11; 2 Corinthians 1:1, 19; Philippians 1:1; 2:19-23; Colossians 1:1; 1 Thessalonians 1:1-10; 2:3-4; 3:2-6; 1 and 2 Timothy; Philemon; Hebrews 13:23.

---

places the primary blame for humanity's sinful nature on Adam (Romans 5:12-21).

2:15 The phrase "saved through childbearing" can be understood several ways: (1) Man sinned, so men were condemned to painful labor. Woman sinned, so women were condemned to pain in childbearing. Both men and women, however, can be saved through trusting Christ and obeying him. (2) Women who fulfill their God-given roles are demonstrating true commitment and obedience to Christ. One of the most important roles for a wife and mother is to care for her family. (3) The childbearing mentioned here refers to the birth of Jesus Christ. Women (and men) are saved spiritually because of the most important birth, that of Christ himself. (4) From the lessons learned through the trials of childbearing, women can develop qualities that teach them about love, trust, submission, and service.

Leaders in the Church

3 This is a trustworthy saying: "If someone aspires to be an elder,* he desires an honorable position." ²So an elder must be a man whose life is above reproach. He must be faithful to his wife.* He must exercise self-control, live wisely, and have a good reputation. He must enjoy having guests in his home, and he must be able to teach. ³He must not be a heavy drinker* or be violent. He must be gentle, not quarrelsome, and not love money. ⁴He must manage his own family well, having children who respect and obey him. ⁵For if a man cannot manage his own household, how can he take care of God's church?

⁶An elder must not be a new believer, because he might become proud, and the devil would cause him to fall.* ⁷Also, people outside the church must speak well of him so that he will not be disgraced and fall into the devil's trap.

⁸In the same way, deacons must be well respected and have integrity. They must not be heavy drinkers or dishonest with money. ⁹They must be committed to the mystery of the faith now revealed and must live with a clear conscience. ¹⁰Before they are appointed as deacons, let them be closely examined. If they pass the test, then let them serve as deacons.

¹¹In the same way, their wives* must be respected and must not slander others. They must exercise self-control and be faithful in everything they do.

¹²A deacon must be faithful to his wife, and he must manage his children and household well. ¹³Those who do well as deacons will be rewarded with respect from others and will have increased confidence in their faith in Christ Jesus.

3:1 Acts 20:28
3:2-7 Titus 1:6-9
3:7 2 Cor 8:21 / 2 Tim 2:26
3:9 1 Tim 1:19

3:1 Or *an overseer,* or *a bishop;* also in 3:2, 6.   **3:2** Or *must have only one wife,* or *must be married only once;* Greek reads *must be the husband of one wife;* also in 3:12.   **3:3** Greek *must not drink too much wine;* similarly in 3:8.
3:6 Or *he might fall into the same judgment as the devil.*   **3:11** Or *the women deacons.* The Greek word can be translated *women* or *wives.*

• **3:1** To be a church leader ("elder") is a heavy responsibility because the church belongs to the living God. The word *elder* can refer to a pastor, church leader, or presiding overseer. It is good to want to be a spiritual leader, but the standards are high. Paul enumerates some of the qualifications here. Church leaders should not be elected because they are popular, nor should they be allowed to push their way to the top. Instead, they should be chosen by the church because of their respect for the truth, both in what they believe and in how they live. Do you hold a position of spiritual leadership, or would you like to be a leader someday? Check yourself against Paul's standard of excellence. Those with great responsibility must meet high expectations.

• **3:1-13** All believers, even if they never plan to be church leaders, should strive to follow these guidelines because they are consistent with what God says is true and right. For example, some people are effectively "able to teach" who never teach or lead formally at church. Their lessons are passed on to one or two others. They become mentors of spiritual truth. Paul described this intimate kind of teaching in 2 Timothy 2:2, "You have heard me teach things that have been confirmed by many reliable witnesses. Now teach these truths to other trustworthy people who are able to pass them on to others." More is learned through living than through lectures. If you have been able to communicate your faith clearly to another person, you have demonstrated teaching at its best. In measuring your ability to teach, don't consider how many students you have had; instead, ask how much truth you have passed on to even one student whom God has brought your way.

• **3:2** Paul's statement that each elder should be faithful to his wife prohibits both polygamy and promiscuity. This does not prohibit an unmarried person from becoming an elder or a widowed elder from remarrying.

• **3:4, 5** Christian workers and volunteers sometimes make the mistake of being so involved in their work that they neglect their families, and especially the firm discipline of their children. Spiritual leadership, however, must begin at home. If a man is not willing to care for, discipline, and teach his children, he is not qualified to lead the church. Don't allow your volunteer activities to detract from your family responsibilities.

3:6 New believers should become secure and strong in the faith before taking leadership roles in the church. Too often, in a church desperate for workers, new believers are placed in positions of responsibility prematurely. New faith needs time to mature. New believers should have a place of service, but they should not be put into leadership positions until they are firmly grounded in their faith, with a solid Christian lifestyle and a knowledge of the Word of God.

3:6 Younger believers who are selected for office need to beware of the damaging effects of pride. Pride can seduce emotions and cloud reason. It can make those who are immature susceptible to the influence of unscrupulous people. Pride and conceit were the devil's downfall, and he uses pride to trap others.

3:7 People outside the church should speak well of those who would lead in the church. The good reputation with outsiders that Paul required is realized when Christians act as dependable friends and good neighbors. How we carry out our duties as citizens, neighbors, and friends facilitates our ability to communicate the gospel. Do you have friends who are not believers? Does your conduct help or hinder the cause of Christ? As the church carries out its mission in an increasingly secular world, the church needs those who build bridges with unbelievers in order to bring them the gospel.

• **3:8-13** *Deacon* means "one who serves." This position was possibly begun by the apostles in the Jerusalem church (Acts 6:1-6) to care for the physical needs of the congregation—at that time, the needs of the Greek-speaking widows. Deacons were leaders in the church, and their qualifications resemble those of the elders. In some churches today, the office of deacon has lost its importance. New Christians are often asked to serve in this position, but that is not the New Testament pattern. Paul says that potential deacons should have high qualifications and be very carefully chosen.

3:11 "Wives" can refer to women helpers or deaconesses. It could also mean wives of deacons or female leaders of the church (such as Phoebe, the deaconess mentioned in Romans 16:1). In either case, Paul expected the behavior of prominent women in the church to be just as responsible and blameless as that of prominent men.

The Truths of Our Faith

3:15
Matt 16:16-18
Eph 2:19-21

[14]I am writing these things to you now, even though I hope to be with you soon, [15]so that if I am delayed, you will know how people must conduct themselves in the household of God. This is the church of the living God, which is the pillar and foundation of the truth.

3:16
Isa 7:14
Matt 4:11
John 1:14
Rom 1:3-4
Acts 1:9
1 Jn 4:2-3; 5:6

[16]Without question, this is the great mystery of our faith*:

Christ* was revealed in a human body
    and vindicated by the Spirit.*
He was seen by angels
    and announced to the nations.
He was believed in throughout the world
    and taken to heaven in glory.

3. Instructions for elders

Warnings against False Teachers

4:1
John 16:13
2 Tim 3:1
2 Pet 3:3

4 Now the Holy Spirit tells us clearly that in the last times some will turn away from the true faith; they will follow deceptive spirits and teachings that come from demons. [2]These people are hypocrites and liars, and their consciences are dead.*

4:2
Eph 4:19

4:3
Gen 9:3
Rom 14:6
1 Cor 10:30-31

[3]They will say it is wrong to be married and wrong to eat certain foods. But God created those foods to be eaten with thanks by faithful people who know the truth. [4]Since everything God created is good, we should not reject any of it but receive it with thanks. [5]For we know it is made acceptable* by the word of God and prayer.

4:4
Gen 1:31
Acts 10:15

A Good Servant of Christ Jesus

4:6
2 Tim 3:15

[6]If you explain these things to the brothers and sisters,* Timothy, you will be a worthy servant of Christ Jesus, one who is nourished by the message of faith and the good teaching you

3:16a Or *of godliness.* **3:16b** Greek *He who;* other manuscripts read *God.* **3:16c** Or *in his spirit.* **4:2** Greek *are seared.* **4:5** Or *made holy.* **4:6** Greek *brothers.*

3:14, 15 The Bible is the written form of what God expects us to know and do. God chose Paul to carry out one phase of the plan. Through Paul, the inspired teaching was written down. As such, it was passed on to Timothy. Then, it was passed on to others. Later, it was passed on to us. Times have changed, but the original authority remains. Because the Bible is from God, it must be studied seriously, understood thoroughly, and applied faithfully. Paul intended this letter to teach believers how to conduct themselves. We would do well to read carefully.

3:16 In this short hymn, Paul affirms the humanity and divinity of Christ. By so doing he reveals the heart of the Good News, "the great mystery of our faith" (the secret of how we become godly). "Revealed in a human body"—Jesus was a man; Jesus' incarnation is the basis of our being right with God. "Vindicated by the Spirit"—Jesus' resurrection showed that the Holy Spirit's power was in him (Romans 8:11). "Seen by angels" and "taken to heaven"—Jesus is divine. We can't please God on our own; we must depend on Christ. As a man, Jesus lived a perfect life, and so he is a perfect example of how to live. As God, Jesus gives us the power to do what is right. It is possible to live a godly life—through following Christ.

4:1 The "last times" began with Christ's resurrection and will continue until his return when he will set up his Kingdom and judge all humanity.

4:1, 2 False teachers were and still are a threat to the church. Jesus and the apostles repeatedly warned against them (see, for example, Mark 13:21-23; Acts 20:28-31; 2 Thessalonians 2:1-12; 2 Peter 3:3-7). It is not enough that a teacher appears to know what he is talking about, is disciplined and moral, or says that he is speaking for God. If his words contradict the Bible, his teaching is false. Like Timothy, we must guard against any teaching that causes believers to dilute or reject any aspect of their faith. Such false teaching can be very direct or extremely subtle. Believers ought to respond quickly when they sense false teaching being promoted. The truth does not mind honest questions. Sometimes the source may prove to be ignorant of the error and appreciate the correction. But a firm warning may at least keep potential

victims from the disastrous results of apostasy that Paul described. For how to spot false teaching, see the note on 1:3-7.

4:1-5 Paul said the false teachers were hypocrites and liars who encouraged people to follow "deceptive spirits and teachings that come from demons." The danger that Timothy faced in Ephesus seems to have come from certain people in the church who were following some Greek philosophers who taught that the body was evil and that only the soul mattered. The false teachers refused to believe that the God of creation was good, because his very contact with the physical world would have soiled him. Though these Greek-influenced church members honored Jesus, they could not believe he was truly human. Paul knew that their teachings, if left unchecked, would greatly distort Christian truth.

Satan deceives people by offering a clever imitation of the real thing. The false teachers gave stringent rules (such as forbidding people to marry or to eat certain foods). This made them appear self-disciplined and righteous. Their strict disciplines for the body, however, could not remove sin (see Colossians 2:20-23). We must not be unduly impressed by a teacher's style or credentials; we must look to his teaching about Jesus Christ. His conclusions about Christ show the source of his message.

4:4, 5 In opposition to the false teachers, Paul affirmed that everything God created is good (see Genesis 1). We should ask for God's blessing on his created gifts that give us pleasure and thank him for them. This doesn't mean that we should abuse what God has made (for example, gluttony abuses God's gift of good food, lust abuses God's gift of love, and murder abuses God's gift of life). Instead of abusing, we should enjoy these gifts by using them to serve and honor God. Have you thanked God for the good gifts he has given? Are you using the gifts in ways pleasing to you *and* to God?

have followed. ⁷Do not waste time arguing over godless ideas and old wives' tales. Instead, train yourself to be godly. ⁸"Physical training is good, but training for godliness is much better, promising benefits in this life and in the life to come." ⁹This is a trustworthy saying, and everyone should accept it. ¹⁰This is why we work hard and continue to struggle,* for our hope is in the living God, who is the Savior of all people and particularly of all believers.

¹¹Teach these things and insist that everyone learn them. ¹²Don't let anyone think less of you because you are young. Be an example to all believers in what you say, in the way you live, in your love, your faith, and your purity. ¹³Until I get there, focus on reading the Scriptures to the church, encouraging the believers, and teaching them.

¹⁴Do not neglect the spiritual gift you received through the prophecy spoken over you when the elders of the church laid their hands on you. ¹⁵Give your complete attention to these matters. Throw yourself into your tasks so that everyone will see your progress. ¹⁶Keep a close watch on how you live and on your teaching. Stay true to what is right for the sake of your own salvation and the salvation of those who hear you.

4:7
1 Tim 1:4
2 Tim 2:16
Titus 1:14
4:8
1 Tim 6:6
4:9
1 Tim 1:15
4:10
1 Tim 2:3-4
4:11
1 Tim 5:7; 6:2
4:12
Titus 2:15
4:13
1 Tim 3:14
4:14
Acts 6:6; 8:17
2 Tim 1:6

Advice about Widows, Elders, and Slaves

5 Never speak harshly to an older man,* but appeal to him respectfully as you would to your own father. Talk to younger men as you would to your own brothers. ²Treat older women as you would your mother, and treat younger women with all purity as you would your own sisters.

³Take care of* any widow who has no one else to care for her. ⁴But if she has children or grandchildren, their first responsibility is to show godliness at home and repay their parents by taking care of them. This is something that pleases God.

5:1
Lev 19:32
Titus 2:2, 6
5:4
Eph 6:2
1 Tim 2:3

4:10 Some manuscripts read *continue to suffer.*   **5:1** Or *an elder.*   **5:3** Or *Honor.*

• **4:7-10** Are you in shape both physically and spiritually? In our society, much emphasis is placed on physical fitness, but spiritual health is even more important. Our physical health is susceptible to disease and injury, but faith can sustain us through any tragedy. To train ourselves to be godly, we must develop our faith by using our God-given abilities in the service of the church (see 4:14-16). Are you developing your spiritual muscles?

4:10 Christ is the Savior for all, but his salvation becomes effective only for those who trust him.

• **4:12** Timothy was a young pastor. It would have been easy for older Christians to look down on him because of his youth. He had to earn the respect of his elders by setting an example in his speech, life, love, faith, and purity. Regardless of your age, God can use you. Whether you are young or old, don't think of your age as a handicap. Live so others can see Christ in you.

4:12-16 Apparently Timothy needed some encouragement. Most likely, so do many people around you. Each day we have many opportunities to support and inspire family members, fellow workers, and even total strangers. People need help and affirmation all along the way. Paul modeled six important principles to help us encourage others: (1) Begin with encouragement. People who know we will encourage them will be happy to work with us. (2) Expect of others only what you expect of yourself. People will resist being held to unfair standards. (3) Develop expectations of others with consideration for their skills, maturity, and experience. People will reject or fail to meet expectations that do not fit them. Be patient with distracted or slow learners. (4) Monitor your expectations of others. Changing circumstances sometimes require revised or reduced expectations. (5) Clarify your expectations with others. People are not likely to hit a target that no one has identified. (6) End with encouragement. People love to be thanked for a job well done.

4:13 The "Scriptures" referred to here are, in fact, the Old Testament. We must make sure to emphasize the entire Bible, both the Old and the New Testaments. There are rich rewards in studying the people, events, prophecies, and principles of the Old Testament.

• **4:14** Highly skilled and talented athletes lose their abilities if their muscles aren't toned by constant use. Likewise, we will lose our spiritual gifts if we don't put them to work. Our talents are improved by exercise, but failing to use them causes them to waste away from lack of practice and nourishment. What gifts and abilities has God given you? Use them regularly in serving God and others. (See Romans 12:1-8; 2 Timothy 1:6-8 for more on using well the abilities God has given us.)

• **4:16** We must be on constant guard against falling into sin that can so easily destroy us. Yet we must watch what we believe ("teaching") just as closely. Wrong beliefs can quickly lead us into sin and heresy. We should be on guard against those who would persuade us that how we live is more important than what we believe. We should keep a close watch on both, staying true to the faith.

• **5:2** Men in the ministry can avoid improper attitudes toward women by treating them as family members. If men see women as fellow members in God's family, they will protect them and help them grow spiritually.

5:3ff Paul wanted Christian families to be as self-supporting as possible. He insisted that children and grandchildren take care of the widows in their families (5:4); he suggested that younger widows remarry and start new families (5:14); he ordered the church not to support lazy members who refused to work (2 Thessalonians 3:10). Nevertheless, when necessary, the believers pooled their resources (Acts 2:44-47); they gave generously to help disaster-ridden churches (1 Corinthians 16:1-4); they took care of a large number of widows (Acts 6:1-6). The church has always had limited resources and has always had to balance financial responsibility with generosity. It only makes sense for members to work as hard as they can and to be as independent as possible, so they can adequately care for themselves and for less fortunate members. When church members are both responsible and generous, everyone's needs will be met.

• **5:3-5** Because there were no pensions, no social security, no life insurance, and few honorable jobs for women, widows were usually unable to support themselves. The responsibility for caring for the helpless naturally falls first on their families—the people whose lives are most closely linked with theirs. Paul stresses the importance of each family caring for the needs of its widows and not leaving it for the church. The church can then care for those widows who have no families. A widow who had no children or

5:5
Luke 2:36-37
1 Pet 3:5

5:6
Luke 15:24
Jas 5:5

⁵Now a true widow, a woman who is truly alone in this world, has placed her hope in God. She prays night and day, asking God for his help. ⁶But the widow who lives only for pleasure is spiritually dead even while she lives. ⁷Give these instructions to the church so that no one will be open to criticism.

⁸But those who won't care for their relatives, especially those in their own household, have denied the true faith. Such people are worse than unbelievers.

5:10
Gen 18:3-5
Acts 9:36

⁹A widow who is put on the list for support must be a woman who is at least sixty years old and was faithful to her husband.* ¹⁰She must be well respected by everyone because of the good she has done. Has she brought up her children well? Has she been kind to strangers and served other believers humbly?* Has she helped those who are in trouble? Has she always been ready to do good?

5:13
2 Thes 3:11

5:14
1 Cor 7:9

5:15
1 Tim 1:19-20

¹¹The younger widows should not be on the list, because their physical desires will overpower their devotion to Christ and they will want to remarry. ¹²Then they would be guilty of breaking their previous pledge. ¹³And if they are on the list, they will learn to be lazy and will spend their time gossiping from house to house, meddling in other people's business and talking about things they shouldn't. ¹⁴So I advise these younger widows to marry again, have children, and take care of their own homes. Then the enemy will not be able to say anything against them. ¹⁵For I am afraid that some of them have already gone astray and now follow Satan.

¹⁶If a woman who is a believer has relatives who are widows, she must take care of them and not put the responsibility on the church. Then the church can care for the widows who are truly alone.

5:17
Phil 2:29
1 Thes 5:12

5:18
†Deut 25:4
Matt 10:10
†Luke 10:7
1 Cor 9:9

¹⁷Elders who do their work well should be respected and paid well,* especially those who work hard at both preaching and teaching. ¹⁸For the Scripture says, "You must not muzzle an ox to keep it from eating as it treads out the grain." And in another place, "Those who work deserve their pay!"*

¹⁹Do not listen to an accusation against an elder unless it is confirmed by two or three

5:19
Matt 18:16

5:9 Greek *was the wife of one husband.*   **5:10** Greek *and washed the feet of God's holy people?*   **5:17** Greek *should be worthy of double honor.*   **5:18** Deut 25:4; Luke 10:7.

---

other family members to support her was doomed to poverty. From the beginning, the church took care of its widows, who in turn gave valuable service to the church.

The church should support those who have no families and should also help the elderly, young, disabled, ill, or poverty-stricken with their emotional and spiritual needs. Often families who are caring for their own helpless members have heavy burdens. They may need extra money, a listening ear, a helping hand, or a word of encouragement. Interestingly, those who are helped often turn around and help others, turning the church into more of a caring community. Don't wait for people to ask. Take the initiative and look for ways to serve them.

• **5:8** Healthy homes remain the best possible training environment for children. When it comes to caring for relatives and honoring parents, children take most of their cues by watching how Mom and Dad honor the grandparents. If our children see the way we, as parents, care for our parents, they will understand the importance of such honor for us in the future. Healthy, practical honor becomes a priceless gift that one generation gives to another. Disrespect and lack of care provide harmful examples that will eventually turn on us. The warning in the verse is ominous indeed.

5:9-16 Apparently some older widows had been "put on the list for support," meaning that they had taken a vow committing themselves to work for the church in exchange for financial support. Paul lists a few qualifications for these church workers: These widows should be at least 60 years old, should have been faithful to their husbands, and should be well known for their kind deeds. Younger widows should not be included in this group because they might desire to marry again and thus have to break their pledge (5:11, 12).

Three out of four wives today eventually are widowed, so many of the older women in our churches have lost their husbands. Does your church provide an avenue of service for these women?

Could you help match their gifts and abilities with your church's needs? Often their maturity and wisdom can be of great service in the church.

5:15 "Gone astray and now follow Satan" refers to the immoral conduct that identified these women with their pagan neighbors.

5:17 Preaching and teaching are closely related. Preaching is proclaiming the Word of God and confronting listeners with the truth of Scripture. Teaching is explaining the truth in Scripture, helping learners understand difficult passages, and helping them apply God's Word to daily life. Paul says that these elders are worthy of double honor. Unfortunately, however, we often take them for granted by not providing adequately for their needs or by subjecting them to heavy criticism. Think of how you can honor your leaders who work hard at preaching and teaching.

5:17, 18 Faithful church leaders should be supported and appreciated. Too often they are targets for criticism because the congregation has unrealistic expectations. How do you treat your church leaders? Do you enjoy finding fault, or do you show your appreciation? Do they receive enough financial support to allow them to live without worry and to provide for the needs of their families? Jesus and Paul emphasized the importance of supporting those who lead and teach us (see Galatians 6:6 and the notes on Luke 10:7 and 1 Corinthians 9:4-10). Our ministers deserve to know that we are giving to them cheerfully, gratefully, and generously.

• **5:19-21** Church leaders are not exempt from sin, faults, and mistakes. But they are often criticized for the wrong reasons— minor imperfections, failure to meet someone's expectations, personality clashes. Thus, Paul said that accusations should not even be heard unless two or three witnesses confirm them. Sometimes church leaders should be confronted about their behavior, and sometimes they should be rebuked. But all rebuking must be done fairly and lovingly and for the purpose of restoration.

witnesses. 20Those who sin should be reprimanded in front of the whole church; this will serve as a strong warning to others.

21I solemnly command you in the presence of God and Christ Jesus and the highest angels to obey these instructions without taking sides or showing favoritism to anyone.

22Never be in a hurry about appointing a church leader.* Do not share in the sins of others. Keep yourself pure.

23Don't drink only water. You ought to drink a little wine for the sake of your stomach because you are sick so often.

24Remember, the sins of some people are obvious, leading them to certain judgment. But there are others whose sins will not be revealed until later. 25In the same way, the good deeds of some people are obvious. And the good deeds done in secret will someday come to light.

6 All slaves should show full respect for their masters so they will not bring shame on the name of God and his teaching. 2If the masters are believers, that is no excuse for being disrespectful. Those slaves should work all the harder because their efforts are helping other believers* who are well loved.

False Teaching and True Riches

Teach these things, Timothy, and encourage everyone to obey them. 3Some people may contradict our teaching, but these are the wholesome teachings of the Lord Jesus Christ. These teachings promote a godly life. 4Anyone who teaches something different is arrogant and lacks understanding. Such a person has an unhealthy desire to quibble over the meaning of words. This stirs up arguments ending in jealousy, division, slander, and evil suspicions. 5These people always cause trouble. Their minds are corrupt, and they have turned their backs on the truth. To them, a show of godliness is just a way to become wealthy.

6Yet true godliness with contentment is itself great wealth. 7After all, we brought nothing with us when we came into the world, and we can't take anything with us when we leave it. 8So if we have enough food and clothing, let us be content.

5:20
Deut 13:11
Eph 5:11

5:21
1 Tim 6:13

5:22
1 Tim 4:14

5:23
1 Tim 3:8

5:24-25
Rev 14:13

6:1
Eph 6:5
Titus 2:9-10

6:2
Phlm 1:16

6:3
1 Tim 1:3, 10

6:4
2 Tim 2:14

6:5
2 Tim 3:8; 4:4
Titus 1:14

6:6
Phil 4:11-12
Heb 13:5

6:7
Eccl 5:15
Job 1:21

6:8
Prov 30:8
Heb 13:5

5:22 Greek *about the laying on of hands.*　6:2 Greek *brothers.*

• **5:21** Church leadership is a heavy responsibility. As difficult as it might be, Timothy was not to waver on any of Paul's instructions (and particularly the instructions about rebuking elders). Any needed discipline or rebuke must be administered without regard to Timothy's personal inclinations or favoritism. Likewise, leadership in the church today must be handled with maturity, faithfulness, godliness, and lack of favoritism. The health of a body of believers is far more important than playing favorites with someone who is not meeting the standards set forth here.

5:22, 24, 25 Paul says that a church should never be in a hurry about choosing its leaders, especially the pastor, because major problems or sins might be overlooked. It is a serious responsibility to choose church leaders. They must have strong faith and be morally upright, having the qualities described in 3:1-13 and Titus 1:5-9. Not everyone who wants to be a church leader is eligible. Be certain of an applicant's qualifications before asking him or her to take a leadership position.

5:23 It is unclear why Paul gave this advice to Timothy. Perhaps contaminated water had led to Timothy's indigestion, and so he should stop drinking only water. Whatever the reason, this statement is not an invitation to overindulgence or alcoholism.

• **6:1, 2** In Paul's culture there was a great social and legal gulf separating masters and slaves. But as Christians, masters and slaves became spiritual equals, brothers and sisters in Christ Jesus (Galatians 3:28). Paul did not speak against the institution of slavery, but he gave guidelines for Christian slaves and Christian masters. His counsel for the master/slave relationship can be applied to the employer/employee relationship today. Employees should work hard, showing respect for their employers. In turn, employers should be fair (Ephesians 6:5-9;

Colossians 3:22–4:15). Our work should reflect our faithfulness to and love for Christ.

• **6:3-5** Paul told Timothy to stay away from those who just wanted to make money from preaching and from those who strayed from the sound teachings of the Good News into quarrels that caused strife in the church. A person's understanding of the finer points of theology should not become the basis for lording it over others or for making money. Stay away from people who just want to argue.

• **6:6** This statement is the key to spiritual growth and personal fulfillment. We should honor God and center our desires on him (Matthew 6:33), and we should be content with what God is doing in our lives (Philippians 4:11-13).

• **6:6-10** Despite overwhelming evidence to the contrary, most people still believe that money brings happiness. Rich people craving greater riches can be caught in an endless cycle that only ends in ruin and destruction. How can you keep away from the love of money? Paul gives us some guidelines: (1) Realize that one day riches will all be gone (6:7, 17); (2) be content with what you have (6:8); (3) monitor what you are willing to do to get more money (6:9, 10); (4) love people more than money (6:11); (5) love God's work more than money (6:11); (6) freely share what you have with others (6:18). (See Proverbs 30:7-9 for more on avoiding the love of money.)

• **6:8, 9** "If we have enough . . . let us be content." But when is *enough* enough? How can we truly be content? There is a difference between what we *need* and what we *want*. We may have all we need to live (that is, we have *enough*), but we let ourselves become anxious and discontent over what we merely want. Like Paul, we can choose to be content without having all that we want. The only alternative is to be "trapped by many foolish and harmful desires" that ultimately lead only to "ruin and destruction."

6:9
Prov 23:4; 28:22

⁹But people who long to be rich fall into temptation and are trapped by many foolish and harmful desires that plunge them into ruin and destruction. ¹⁰For the love of money is the root of all kinds of evil. And some people, craving money, have wandered from the true faith and pierced themselves with many sorrows.

Paul's Final Instructions

6:11
2 Tim 2:22

6:12
1 Cor 9:25-26
2 Tim 4:7

6:13
John 18:33-37

6:14
1 Thes 3:13

6:15
Deut 10:17
1 Tim 1:17
Rev 17:14

6:16
Exod 33:20
Ps 104:2
John 1:18; 5:26
1 Tim 1:17

6:17
Luke 12:20-21

6:19
Matt 6:20
1 Tim 6:12

6:20
2 Tim 1:14; 2:16

6:21
2 Tim 2:18

¹¹But you, Timothy, are a man of God; so run from all these evil things. Pursue righteousness and a godly life, along with faith, love, perseverance, and gentleness. ¹²Fight the good fight for the true faith. Hold tightly to the eternal life to which God has called you, which you have confessed so well before many witnesses. ¹³And I charge you before God, who gives life to all, and before Christ Jesus, who gave a good testimony before Pontius Pilate, ¹⁴that you obey this command without wavering. Then no one can find fault with you from now until our Lord Jesus Christ comes again. ¹⁵For at just the right time Christ will be revealed from heaven by the blessed and only almighty God, the King of all kings and Lord of all lords. ¹⁶He alone can never die, and he lives in light so brilliant that no human can approach him. No human eye has ever seen him, nor ever will. All honor and power to him forever! Amen.

¹⁷Teach those who are rich in this world not to be proud and not to trust in their money, which is so unreliable. Their trust should be in God, who richly gives us all we need for our enjoyment. ¹⁸Tell them to use their money to do good. They should be rich in good works and generous to those in need, always being ready to share with others. ¹⁹By doing this they will be storing up their treasure as a good foundation for the future so that they may experience true life.

²⁰Timothy, guard what God has entrusted to you. Avoid godless, foolish discussions with those who oppose you with their so-called knowledge. ²¹Some people have wandered from the faith by following such foolishness.

May God's grace be with you all.

• **6:11, 12** Paul uses active and forceful verbs to describe the Christian life: run, pursue, fight, hold tightly. Some think Christianity is a passive religion that advocates waiting for God to act. On the contrary, we must have an *active* faith, training, working hard, sacrificing, and doing what we know is right. Is it time for action on your part? Christian service, like athletics, requires training and sacrifice. Our discipline and obedience largely define whether or not we will be contributors or merely spectators. How would other believers rank your contributing role on Christ's team?

6:13 Jesus' trial before Pilate is recorded in the Gospels: Matthew 27:11-26; Mark 15:1-15; Luke 23:1-25; John 18:28–19:16.

• **6:17-19** Ephesus was a wealthy city, and the Ephesian church probably had many wealthy members. Paul advised Timothy to deal with any potential problems by teaching that having riches carries great responsibility. If you have been blessed with wealth, then thank the Lord. Don't be proud and don't trust in your money. Use your money to do good. Be rich in good works, generous, and ready to share. No matter how much money you have, your life should demonstrate that God controls the wealth that he has placed under your care.

6:21 The book of 1 Timothy provides guiding principles for local churches, including rules for public worship and qualifications for elders (overseers, pastors), deacons, and special church workers (widows). Paul tells the church leaders to correct incorrect doctrine and to deal lovingly and fairly with all people in the church. The church is not organized simply for the sake of organization but so that Christ can be honored and glorified. While studying these guidelines, don't lose sight of what is most important in the life of the church—knowing God, working together in loving harmony, and taking God's Good News to the world.

2 TIMOTHY

VITAL STATISTICS

PURPOSE:
To give final instructions and encouragement to Timothy, pastor of the church at Ephesus

AUTHOR:
Paul

ORIGINAL AUDIENCE:
Timothy

DATE WRITTEN:
Approximately A.D. 66 or 67, from prison in Rome. After a year or two of freedom, Paul was arrested again and executed under Emperor Nero.

SETTING:
Paul was virtually alone in prison; only Luke was with him. Paul wrote this letter to pass the torch to the new generation of church leaders. He also asked for visits from his friends and for his books, especially the papers—possibly parts of the Old Testament, the Gospels, and other biblical manuscripts.

KEY VERSE:
"Work hard so you can present yourself to God and receive his approval. Be a good worker, one who does not need to be ashamed and who correctly explains the word of truth" (2:15).

KEY PEOPLE:
Paul, Timothy, Luke, Mark, and others

KEY PLACES:
Rome, Ephesus

SPECIAL FEATURES:
Because this is Paul's last letter, it reveals his heart and his priorities—sound doctrine, steadfast faith, confident endurance, and lasting love.

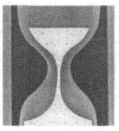

"FAMOUS last words" is more than a cliché. When notable men and women of influence are about to die, the world waits to hear their final words of insight and wisdom. Then those quotes are repeated worldwide. This is also true with a dying loved one. Gathered at his or her side, the family strains to hear every whispered syllable of blessing, encouragement, and advice, knowing that this will be the final message.

One of the most knowledgeable, influential, and beloved men of history is the apostle Paul. And we have his famous last words.

Paul was facing death. He was not dying of a disease in a sterile hospital with loved ones gathered nearby. He was very much alive, but his condition was terminal. Convicted as a follower of Jesus of Nazareth, Paul sat in a cold Roman prison, cut off from the world, with just a visitor or two and his writing materials. Paul knew that soon he would be executed (4:6), so he wrote his final thoughts to his "son" Timothy, passing to him the torch of leadership, reminding him of what was truly important, and encouraging him in the faith. Imagine how Timothy must have read and reread every word; this was the last message from his beloved mentor, Paul. Because of the situation and the recipient, this is the most intimate and moving of all Paul's letters and his last.

Paul's introduction is tender, and every phrase exudes the love he has for Timothy (1:1–5). He then reminds Timothy of the qualities necessary for a faithful minister of Jesus Christ (1:6—2:13). Timothy should remember his call and use his gifts with boldness (1:6–12), keep to the truth (1:13–18), prepare others to follow him in the ministry (2:1, 2), be disciplined and ready to endure suffering (2:3–7), and keep his eyes and mind focused on Christ (2:8–13). Paul challenges Timothy to hold to sound doctrine, reject error and avoid foolish talk, correctly explain the word of truth (2:14–19), and keep his life pure (2:20–26).

Next, Paul warns Timothy of the opposition that he and other believers would face in the last days from self-centered people who use the church for their own gain and teach false doctrines (3:1–9). Paul tells Timothy to be prepared for these unfaithful people by remembering his example (3:10, 11), understanding the real source of the opposition (3:12, 13), and finding strength and power in the Word of God (3:14–17). Then Paul gives Timothy a stirring charge: to preach the Word (4:1–4) and to fulfill his ministry until the end (4:5–8).

Paul concludes with personal requests and items of information. In these final words, he reveals his loneliness and his strong love for his brothers and sisters in Christ (4:9–22).

There has never been another person like Paul, the missionary apostle. He was a man of deep faith, undying love, constant hope, tenacious conviction, and profound insight. And he was inspired by the Holy Spirit to give us God's message. As you read 2 Timothy, know that you are reading the last words of this great man of God—his last words to Timothy and to all who would claim to follow Christ. Recommit yourself to stand courageously for the truth, knowing the Word and being empowered by the Holy Spirit.

THE BLUEPRINT

1. Foundations of Christian service
   (1:1—2:26)
2. Difficult times for Christian service
   (3:1—4:22)

Paul gives helpful advice to Timothy to remain solidly grounded in Christian service and to endure suffering during the difficult days to come. It is easy for us to serve Christ for the wrong reasons: because it is exciting, rewarding, or personally enriching. Without a proper foundation, however, we will find it easy to quit during difficult times. All believers need a strong foundation for their service, because Christian service does not get easier as we grow older, and it will become no easier as the time of Christ's return grows closer.

MEGATHEMES

THEME	EXPLANATION	IMPORTANCE
Boldness	In the face of opposition and persecution, Timothy was to carry out his ministry without fear or shame. Paul urged him to utilize boldly the gifts of preaching and teaching that the Holy Spirit had given him.	The Holy Spirit helps us to be wise and strong. God honors our confident testimony even when we suffer. To get over our fear of what people might say or do, we must take our eyes off of people and look only to God.
Faithfulness	Christ was faithful to all of us in dying for our sin. Paul was a faithful minister even when he was in prison. Paul urged Timothy to maintain not only sound doctrine but also loyalty, diligence, and endurance.	We can count on opposition, suffering, and hardship as we serve Christ. But this shows that our faithfulness is having an effect on others. As we trust Christ, he counts us worthy to suffer, and he will give us the strength we need to be steadfast.
Preaching and Teaching	Paul and Timothy were active in preaching and teaching the Good News about Jesus Christ. Paul encouraged Timothy not only to carry the torch of truth but also to train others, passing on to them sound doctrine and enthusiasm for Christ's mission.	We must prepare people to transmit God's Word to others so that they in turn might pass it on. Does your church carefully train others to teach?
Error	In the final days before Christ returns, there will be false teachers, spiritual dropouts, and heretics. The remedy for error is to have a solid program for teaching Christians.	Because of deception and false teaching, we must be disciplined and ready to reject error. Know the Word of God as your sure defense against error and confusion.

1. Foundations of Christian service

Greetings from Paul

1:1
John 5:24
Titus 1:1
1 Jn 5:10-11, 20

1:2
1 Tim 1:2

1 This letter is from Paul, chosen by the will of God to be an apostle of Christ Jesus. I have been sent out to tell others about the life he has promised through faith in Christ Jesus. ²I am writing to Timothy, my dear son.

May God the Father and Christ Jesus our Lord give you grace, mercy, and peace.

1:1 This letter has a somber tone. Paul had been imprisoned for the last time, and he knew he would soon die. Unlike Paul's first imprisonment in Rome, when he was in a house (Acts 28:16, 23, 30) where he continued to teach, this time he was probably confined to a cold dungeon, awaiting his death (4:6-8). Emperor Nero had begun a major persecution in A.D. 64 as part of his plan to pass the blame for the great fire of Rome from himself to the Christians. This persecution spread across the empire and included social ostracism, public torture, and murder. As Paul was waiting to die, he wrote a letter to his dear friend Timothy, a younger man who was like a son to him (1:2). Written in approximately A.D. 66/67, these are the last words we have from Paul.

1:1 When we are united with Christ, life takes on both immediate and eternal dimensions. Paul's use of the phrase, "life he has promised," can apply to the life that Jesus gives immediately to those who trust him, as well as to the life fully realized in eternity.

On one hand, Paul said, "Anyone who belongs to Christ has become a new person" (2 Corinthians 5:17). So new life begins at conversion. Yet on the other hand, we "wait with eager hope for the day when God will give us our full rights as his adopted children, including the new bodies he has promised us" (Romans 8:23). The present experience we enjoy provides a foretaste of our complete redemption at Christ's return. When we struggle with difficulties in this life, remember that the best is yet to come.

1:2 Paul's second letter to Timothy was written about two to four years after his first letter. Timothy had been Paul's traveling companion on the second and third missionary journeys, and Paul had left him in Ephesus to help the church there (1 Timothy 1:3, 4). For more information on Timothy, see his Profile in 1 Timothy 2, p. 2059. For more information on the great missionary Paul, see his Profile in Acts 9, p. 1837.

Encouragement to Be Faithful

³Timothy, I thank God for you—the God I serve with a clear conscience, just as my ancestors did. Night and day I constantly remember you in my prayers. ⁴I long to see you again, for I remember your tears as we parted. And I will be filled with joy when we are together again.

⁵I remember your genuine faith, for you share the faith that first filled your grandmother Lois and your mother, Eunice. And I know that same faith continues strong in you. ⁶This is why I remind you to fan into flames the spiritual gift God gave you when I laid my hands on you. ⁷For God has not given us a spirit of fear and timidity, but of power, love, and self-discipline.

⁸So never be ashamed to tell others about our Lord. And don't be ashamed of me, either, even though I'm in prison for him. With the strength God gives you, be ready to suffer with me for the sake of the Good News. ⁹For God saved us and called us to live a holy life. He did this, not because we deserved it, but because that was his plan from before the beginning of time—to show us his grace through Christ Jesus. ¹⁰And now he has made all of this plain to us by the appearing of Christ Jesus, our Savior. He broke the power of death and illuminated the way to life and immortality through the Good News. ¹¹And God chose me to be a preacher, an apostle, and a teacher of this Good News.

¹²That is why I am suffering here in prison. But I am not ashamed of it, for I know the one in whom I trust, and I am sure that he is able to guard what I have entrusted to him* until the day of his return.

1:12 Or *what has been entrusted to me.*

1:4 Acts 20:37
2 Tim 4:9
1:5 Acts 16:1
1:6 1 Tim 4:14
1:7 Rom 8:15
1:8 Rom 1:16
Eph 3:1
2 Tim 2:3
1:9 Rom 8:28; 11:14
Eph 2:8-9
Titus 3:5
1:10 1 Cor 15:54
1:11 1 Tim 2:7
1:12 1 Tim 6:20

1:3 Paul consistently prayed for Timothy, his friend, his fellow traveler, his son in the faith, and a strong leader in the Christian church. Although the two men were separated from each other, their prayers provided a source of mutual encouragement. We, too, should pray consistently for others, especially for those who do God's work. On your prayer list, include your pastor, other church leaders, and missionaries around the world. They need your prayers.

1:4 We don't know when Paul and Timothy last parted, but it was probably when Paul was arrested and taken to Rome for his second imprisonment. The tears they shed at parting revealed the depth of their relationship.

1:5 Timothy's mother and grandmother, Eunice and Lois, were early Christian converts, possibly through Paul's ministry in their home city, Lystra (Acts 16:1). They had communicated their strong Christian faith to Timothy, even though his father was probably not a believer. Don't hide your light at home; our families are fertile fields for planting seeds of the Good News. Let your parents, children, spouse, brothers, and sisters know of your faith in Jesus, and be sure they see Christ's love, helpfulness, and joy in you.

● **1:6** At the time of his ordination, Timothy had received special gifts of the Spirit to enable him to serve the church (see 1 Timothy 4:14). In telling Timothy to "fan into flames the spiritual gift God gave you," Paul was encouraging him to persevere. Timothy did not need new revelations or new gifts; he needed the courage and self-discipline to hang on to the truth and to use the gifts he had already received (see 1:13, 14). If Timothy would step out boldly in faith and proclaim the Good News once again, the Holy Spirit would go with him and give him power. When you use the gifts God has given you, you will find that God will give you the power you need to accomplish whatever task he gives you.

1:6 Clearly Timothy's spiritual gift had been given to him when Paul and the elders had laid their hands on him and set him apart for ministry (see 1 Timothy 4:14). God gives all Christians gifts to use to build up the body of Christ (see 1 Corinthians 12:4-31), and he gives special gifts to some through church leaders, who serve as God's instruments.

● **1:6, 7** Timothy was experiencing great opposition to his message and to himself as a leader. His youth, his association with Paul, and his leadership had come under fire from believers and nonbelievers alike. Paul urged him to be bold. When we allow people to intimidate us, we neutralize our effectiveness for God. The power of the Holy Spirit can help us overcome our fear of

what some might say or do to us so that we can continue to do God's work.

● **1:7** Paul mentions three characteristics of the effective Christian leader: power, love, and self-discipline. These are available to us because the Holy Spirit lives in us. Follow his leading each day so that your life will more fully exhibit these characteristics. See Galatians 5:22, 23 for a list of the by-products of the Holy Spirit living in us.

1:8 In this time of mounting persecution, Timothy may have been afraid to continue preaching the Good News. His fears were based on fact because believers were being arrested and executed. Paul told Timothy to expect suffering—Timothy, like Paul, would be jailed for preaching the Good News (Hebrews 13:23). But Paul promised Timothy that God would give him strength and that he would be ready when it was his turn to suffer. Even when there is no persecution, sharing our faith in Christ can be difficult. Fortunately we, like Paul and Timothy, can rely on the Holy Spirit to give us courage. Don't be ashamed to testify of your personal faith in Jesus Christ.

1:9, 10 In these verses Paul gives a brief summary of the Good News. God loves us, chose us, and sent Christ to die for us. We can have eternal life through faith in him because he broke the power of death with his resurrection. We do not deserve to be saved, but God offers us salvation anyway. What we must do is believe in him and accept his offer.

1:12 In spite of the suffering that might have caused Paul to despair, he affirmed his confidence in God's protection. This was not a claim to strong faith; rather, it was a trust in one so powerful that even a weak faith was sufficient. Paul based his confidence in Christ on his intimate relationship with him. Paul's knew the one in whom he trusted with personal knowledge; he knew Christ so well that no earthly experience could break the bond of love by which Christ held him. If your situation looks bleak, give your concerns to Christ because you know him and love him. Realize that he will guard all you have entrusted to him until the day of his return. For more on our security in Christ, see Romans 8:38, 39.

1:12 The phrase "guard what I have entrusted to him" could mean: (1) Paul knew that God would protect the souls of those converted through his preaching; (2) Paul trusted God to guard his own soul until Christ's second coming; or (3) Paul was confident that, though he was in prison and facing death, God would carry out the Good News ministry through others such as Timothy. Paul may have expressed his confidence to encourage Timothy, who

1:13
Rom 6:17
1 Tim 1:14

1:14
Rom 8:9, 11, 16
Gal 4:6

1:15
2 Tim 4:10, 16

1:16
2 Tim 4:19

1:18
Heb 6:10

2:1
Eph 6:10

2:2
2 Tim 1:13

2:3
2 Tim 1:8; 4:5

2:5
1 Cor 9:25

2:6
1 Cor 9:7, 10

2:8
Acts 2:24
Rom 1:3

2:9
Eph 3:1
Phil 1:12-14

¹³Hold on to the pattern of wholesome teaching you learned from me—a pattern shaped by the faith and love that you have in Christ Jesus. ¹⁴Through the power of the Holy Spirit who lives within us, carefully guard the precious truth that has been entrusted to you.

¹⁵As you know, everyone from the province of Asia has deserted me—even Phygelus and Hermogenes.

¹⁶May the Lord show special kindness to Onesiphorus and all his family because he often visited and encouraged me. He was never ashamed of me because I was in chains. ¹⁷When he came to Rome, he searched everywhere until he found me. ¹⁸May the Lord show him special kindness on the day of Christ's return. And you know very well how helpful he was in Ephesus.

A Good Soldier of Christ Jesus

2 Timothy, my dear son, be strong through the grace that God gives you in Christ Jesus. ²You have heard me teach things that have been confirmed by many reliable witnesses. Now teach these truths to other trustworthy people who will be able to pass them on to others.

³Endure suffering along with me, as a good soldier of Christ Jesus. ⁴Soldiers don't get tied up in the affairs of civilian life, for then they cannot please the officer who enlisted them. ⁵And athletes cannot win the prize unless they follow the rules. ⁶And hardworking farmers should be the first to enjoy the fruit of their labor. ⁷Think about what I am saying. The Lord will help you understand all these things.

⁸Always remember that Jesus Christ, a descendant of King David, was raised from the dead. This is the Good News I preach. ⁹And because I preach this Good News, I am suffering

---

was undoubtedly discouraged by the problems in Ephesus and fearful of persecution. Even in prison, Paul knew that God was still in control. No matter what setbacks or problems we face, we can trust fully in God.

1:13, 14 Timothy was in a time of transition. He had been Paul's bright young helper; soon he would be on his own as leader of a church in a difficult environment. Although his responsibilities were changing, Timothy was not without help. He had everything he needed to face the future if he would hold on tightly to the Lord's resources. When you are facing difficult transitions, follow Paul's advice to Timothy and look back at your experience. Who is the foundation of your faith? How can you build on that foundation? What gifts has the Holy Spirit given you? Use the gifts you have been given.

1:15, 16 Nothing more is known about Phygelus and Hermogenes, who evidently opposed Paul's ministry. These men serve as a warning that even leaders can fall. Onesiphorus was mentioned as a positive example in contrast to these men.

2:1 How can someone be strong through grace? Grace is God's undeserved favor on our behalf. Just as we are saved by God's grace (Ephesians 2:8, 9), we should live by it (Colossians 2:6). This means trusting completely in Christ and *his* power, and not trying to live for Christ in our strength alone. Receive and utilize Christ's power. He will give you the strength to do his work.

2:2 If the church were to consistently follow this advice, it would expand geometrically as well-taught believers would teach others and commission them, in turn, to teach still others. Disciples need to be equipped to pass on their faith; our work is not done until new believers are able to make disciples of others (see Ephesians 4:12, 13).

2:3 The body of Christ contains all believers who have ever lived, not just those who are alive now. When we suffer, we share in a common experience, not just with those alive today, but with all those who have ever suffered for the sake of the gospel. All the martyrs, missionaries, and pioneers of the faith had to face what we face. Let us have the same courage, commitment, and willingness to renounce worldly pleasure in order to serve God. Can you face the challenge? "Therefore, since we are surrounded by such a huge crowd of witnesses to the life of faith, let us strip off every weight that slows us down, especially the sin that so easily trips us up. And let us run with endurance the race God has set before us" (Hebrews 12:1).

● **2:3-7** As Timothy preached and taught, he would face suffering, but he should be able to endure. Paul used comparisons with soldiers, athletes, and farmers who must discipline themselves and be willing to sacrifice to achieve the results they want. Like soldiers, we have to give up worldly security and endure rigorous discipline. Like athletes, we must train hard and follow the rules. Like farmers, we must work extremely hard and be patient. But we keep going despite suffering because of the thought of victory, the vision of winning, and the hope of harvest. We will see that our suffering is worthwhile when we achieve our goal of glorifying God, winning people to Christ, and one day living eternally with him.

2:7 Paul told Timothy to think about his words, and God would give him understanding. God speaks through the Bible, his Word, but we need to be open and receptive to him. As you read the Bible, ask God to show you his timeless truths and their application to your life. Then consider what you have read by thinking it through and meditating on it. God will give you understanding.

2:8 False teachers were a problem in Ephesus (see Acts 20:29, 30; 1 Timothy 1:3-11). At the heart of false teaching is an incorrect view of Christ. In Timothy's day many asserted that Christ was divine but not human—God but not man. These days we often hear that Jesus was human but not divine—man but not God. Either view destroys the good news that Jesus Christ has taken our sins on himself and has reconciled us to God. In this verse, Paul firmly states that Jesus is fully man ("a descendant of King David") and fully God ("raised from the dead"). This is an important doctrine for all Christians. For more on this key concept, see the note on Philippians 2:5-7.

2:9 Paul was in chains in prison because of the Good News he preached. The truth about Jesus is no more popular in our day than in Paul's, but it still reaches receptive hearts. When Paul said that Jesus was God, he angered the Jews who had condemned Jesus for blasphemy; many Jews, however, became followers of Christ (1 Corinthians 1:24). He angered the Romans who worshiped the emperor as god, but even some in Caesar's household turned to Jesus (Philippians 4:22). When Paul said Jesus was human, he angered the Greeks, who thought divinity was soiled if it had any contact with humanity; still, many Greeks accepted the faith (Acts 11:20, 21). The truth that Jesus is one person with two united natures has never been easy to understand, but that doesn't make it untrue. The truth of God's Word is being believed by people every day and changing their lives for eternity. Despite the opposition, continue to proclaim Christ. Some will listen and believe.

and have been chained like a criminal. But the word of God cannot be chained. [10]So I am willing to endure anything if it will bring salvation and eternal glory in Christ Jesus to those God has chosen.

2:10
Col 1:24

[11]This is a trustworthy saying:

2:11
Rom 6:2-11
1 Thes 5:10

If we die with him,
    we will also live with him.
[12] If we endure hardship,
    we will reign with him.
If we deny him,
    he will deny us.

2:12
Matt 10:33
Rom 8:17
1 Pet 4:13

[13] If we are unfaithful,
    he remains faithful,
    for he cannot deny who he is.

2:13
Num 23:19
Rom 3:3
1 Cor 1:9

[14]Remind everyone about these things, and command them in God's presence to stop fighting over words. Such arguments are useless, and they can ruin those who hear them.

2:14
1 Tim 1:4; 6:4
Titus 3:9

An Approved Worker

[15]Work hard so you can present yourself to God and receive his approval. Be a good worker, one who does not need to be ashamed and who correctly explains the word of truth. [16]Avoid worthless, foolish talk that only leads to more godless behavior. [17]This kind of talk spreads like cancer,* as in the case of Hymenaeus and Philetus. [18]They have left the path of truth, claiming that the resurrection of the dead has already occurred; in this way, they have turned some people away from the faith.

2:17
1 Tim 1:20

2:18
1 Tim 1:19; 6:21

2:19
†Num 16:5
Isa 52:11
John 10:14

[19]But God's truth stands firm like a foundation stone with this inscription: "The LORD knows those who are his,"* and "All who belong to the LORD must turn away from evil."*

[20]In a wealthy home some utensils are made of gold and silver, and some are made of

2:20
Rom 9:21

2:17 Greek *gangrene*.   2:19a Num 16:5.   2:19b See Isa 52:11.

2:11-13 This is probably an early Christian hymn. God is faithful to his children. Although we may suffer great hardships here, God promises that someday we will live eternally with him. What will this involve? It means believers will live in Christ's Kingdom, and that we will share in the administration of that Kingdom. This truth comforted Paul as he went through suffering and death. Are you facing hardships? Don't turn away from God— he promises you a wonderful future with him. For more information about living eternally with God, see Matthew 16:24-27; 19:28-30; Luke 22:28-30; Romans 5:17; 6:8; 8:10, 11, 17; 1 Corinthians 15:42-58; Colossians 3:3, 4; 1 Thessalonians 4:13-18; Revelation 3:21; 21:1–22:21.

2:13 Jesus is faithful. He will stay by our side even when we have endured so much that we seem to have no faith left. We may be faithless at times, but Jesus is faithful to his promise to be with us "to the end of the age" (Matthew 28:20). Refusing Christ's help will break our communication with God, but he will never turn his back on us even though we may turn our back on him.

2:14-16 Paul urged Timothy to remind the believers not to argue over unimportant details ("fighting over words") or have foolish discussions because such arguments are confusing, useless, and even harmful. False teachers loved to cause strife and divisions by their meaningless quibbling over unimportant details (see 1 Timothy 6:3-5). To explain the word of truth correctly, we must study what the Word of God says so we can understand what it means.

• **2:15** Because God will examine what kind of workers we have been for him, we should build our lives on his Word and build his Word into our lives. It alone tells us how to live for him and serve him. Believers who ignore the Bible will certainly be ashamed at the judgment. Consistent and diligent study of God's Word is vital; otherwise we will be lulled into neglecting God and our true purpose for living.

• **2:16** In important areas of Christian teaching, we must carefully work through our disagreements. But when we bicker long hours

over words and theories that are not central to the Christian faith and life, we only provoke anger and hurt feelings. Even if "foolish talk" reaches a resolution, it gains little ground for the Kingdom. Learning and discussing are not bad unless they keep believers constantly focusing on false doctrine or unhelpful trivialities. Don't let anything keep you from your work for and service to God.

2:17, 18 Hymenaeus was also mentioned in 1 Timothy 1:20. Paul had turned Hymenaeus over to Satan because his false teaching concerning the resurrection was destroying some people's faith.

2:18 The false teachers were denying the resurrection of the body. They believed that when a person became a Christian, he or she was spiritually reborn, and that was the only resurrection there would ever be. To them, resurrection was symbolic and spiritual, not physical. Paul clearly taught, however, that believers will be resurrected after they die, and that their bodies as well as their souls will live eternally with Christ (1 Corinthians 15:35ff; 2 Corinthians 5:1-10; 1 Thessalonians 4:15-18). We should not try to shape the doctrines of Scripture to match our opinions. If we do, we are putting ourselves above God. Instead, our beliefs should be consistent with God's Word.

2:19 False teachers still spout lies. Some distort the truth, some dilute it, and some simply delete it by saying that God's truth no longer applies. But no matter how many people follow the liars, the solid foundation of God's truth never changes, is never shaken, and will never fade. When we follow God's truth, we will live God's way.

• **2:20, 21** Here Paul urged Timothy to be the kind of person Christ could use for his noblest purposes. Don't settle for less than God's highest and best. Allow him to use you as an instrument of his will. You do this by staying close to him and keeping yourself pure so that sin and its consequences do not get in the way of what God could do in your life. While God can redeem any situation, how much better it is to stay close to Christ and ready to be used by him at a moment's notice.

2:21
2 Tim 3:17

2:22
1 Tim 6:11

2:23
1 Tim 4:7

2:24
1 Tim 3:2-3
Titus 1:7

2:26
1 Tim 3:7

3:1
1 Tim 4:1
Jude 1:18

3:2-3
Rom 1:29-31

3:6
Jude 1:4

wood and clay. The expensive utensils are used for special occasions, and the cheap ones are for everyday use. 21If you keep yourself pure, you will be a special utensil for honorable use. Your life will be clean, and you will be ready for the Master to use you for every good work.

22Run from anything that stimulates youthful lusts. Instead, pursue righteous living, faithfulness, love, and peace. Enjoy the companionship of those who call on the Lord with pure hearts.

23Again I say, don't get involved in foolish, ignorant arguments that only start fights. 24A servant of the Lord must not quarrel but must be kind to everyone, be able to teach, and be patient with difficult people. 25Gently instruct those who oppose the truth. Perhaps God will change those people's hearts, and they will learn the truth. 26Then they will come to their senses and escape from the devil's trap. For they have been held captive by him to do whatever he wants.

2. Difficult times for Christian service
The Dangers of the Last Days

3 You should know this, Timothy, that in the last days there will be very difficult times. 2For people will love only themselves and their money. They will be boastful and proud, scoffing at God, disobedient to their parents, and ungrateful. They will consider nothing sacred. 3They will be unloving and unforgiving; they will slander others and have no self-control. They will be cruel and hate what is good. 4They will betray their friends, be reckless, be puffed up with pride, and love pleasure rather than God. 5They will act religious, but they will reject the power that could make them godly. Stay away from people like that!

6They are the kind who work their way into people's homes and win the confidence of* vulnerable women who are burdened with the guilt of sin and controlled by various desires. 7(Such women are forever following new teachings, but they are never able to understand

3:6 Greek *and take captive.*

2:22 Running away is sometimes considered cowardly. But wise people realize that removing themselves physically from temptation often can be the most courageous action to take. Timothy, a young man, was warned to run from anything that produced evil thoughts. Do you have a recurring temptation that you find difficult to resist? Remove yourself physically from any situation that stimulates your desire to sin. Knowing when to run is as important in spiritual battle as knowing when and how to fight. (See also 1 Timothy 6:11.)

2:23-26 As a teacher, Timothy helped those who were confused about the truth. Paul's advice to Timothy, and to all who teach God's truth, is to be kind and gentle, patiently and courteously explaining the truth. Good teaching never promotes quarrels or foolish arguments. Whether you are teaching Sunday school, leading a Bible study, or preaching in church, remember to listen to people's questions and treat them respectfully, while avoiding foolish debates. If you do this, those who oppose you will be more willing to hear what you have to say and perhaps turn from their error.

3:1 Paul's reference to the "last days" reveals his sense of urgency. The last days began after Jesus' resurrection when the Holy Spirit came upon the believers at Pentecost. The "last days" will continue until Christ's second coming. This means that *we* are living in the last days. So we should make the most of the time that God has given us (Ephesians 5:16; Colossians 4:5).

• **3:1ff** In many parts of the world today, being a Christian is not especially difficult—people aren't jailed for reading the Bible or executed for preaching Christ. (However, this kind of persecution is very real for many believers.) Paul's descriptive list of behavior in the last days describes our society—even, unfortunately, the behavior of many Christians. Check your life against Paul's list. Don't give in to society's pressures. Don't settle for comfort without commitment. Stand up against evil by living as God would have his people live.

3:4 Why is it so tempting to "love pleasure rather than God"? Pleasure is something we can control; God cannot be controlled.

Most pleasures can be obtained easily; love for God requires effort and sometimes sacrifice. Pleasure benefits us now; the benefits of loving God are often in the future. Pleasure has a narcotic effect; it takes our minds off ourselves and our problems. Love for God reminds us of our needs and our responsibilities. Pleasure cooperates with pride. It makes us feel good when we look good in the eyes of others. To love God we must lay aside our pride and our accomplishments. Have you chosen to love pleasure, or to love God? How do you know?

• **3:5** The "act" or appearance of being religious includes going to church, knowing Christian doctrine, using Christian clichés, and following a community's Christian traditions. Such practices can make a person look good, but if the inner attitudes of belief, love, and worship are lacking, the outer appearance is meaningless. Paul warns us not to be deceived by people who only appear to be Christians. It may be difficult to distinguish them from true Christians at first, but their daily behavior will give them away. The characteristics described in 3:2-4 are unmistakable.

3:6, 7 Because of their cultural background, women in the Ephesian church had received no formal religious training. They enjoyed their new freedom to study Christian truths, but their eagerness to learn made them a target for false teachers. Paul warned Timothy to watch out for men who would take advantage of these women. New believers need to grow in their knowledge of the Word because ignorance can make them vulnerable to deception.

3:7 This verse is not opposing study and learning; it is warning about ineffective learning. It is possible to be a perpetual student and never graduate to putting theory into practice. But honest seekers and true students look for answers. Remember this as you study God's Word. Seek to find God's truth and will for your life. Then do as he says.

the truth.) 8These teachers oppose the truth just as Jannes and Jambres opposed Moses. They have depraved minds and a counterfeit faith. 9But they won't get away with this for long. Someday everyone will recognize what fools they are, just as with Jannes and Jambres.

3:8
1 Tim 6:5

Paul's Charge to Timothy

10But you, Timothy, certainly know what I teach, and how I live, and what my purpose in life is. You know my faith, my patience, my love, and my endurance. 11You know how much persecution and suffering I have endured. You know all about how I was persecuted in Antioch, Iconium, and Lystra—but the Lord rescued me from all of it. 12Yes, and everyone who wants to live a godly life in Christ Jesus will suffer persecution. 13But evil people and impostors will flourish. They will deceive others and will themselves be deceived.

14But you must remain faithful to the things you have been taught. You know they are true, for you know you can trust those who taught you. 15You have been taught the holy Scriptures from childhood, and they have given you the wisdom to receive the salvation that comes by trusting in Christ Jesus. 16All Scripture is inspired by God and is useful to teach us what is true and to make us realize what is wrong in our lives. It corrects us when we are wrong and teaches us to do what is right. 17God uses it to prepare and equip his people to do every good work.

3:10
1 Tim 4:6
3:11
Ps 34:19
Acts 13:14, 50-51;
14:5, 19
3:12
John 15:20
Acts 14:22
3:14
2 Tim 1:13; 2:2
3:15
John 5:39
3:16
Rom 15:4
2 Pet 1:20-21
3:17
1 Tim 6:11
2 Tim 2:21

4 I solemnly urge you in the presence of God and Christ Jesus, who will someday judge the living and the dead when he appears to set up his Kingdom: 2Preach the word of God. Be prepared, whether the time is favorable or not. Patiently correct, rebuke, and encourage your people with good teaching.

4:1
Acts 10:42
4:2
1 Tim 5:20
Titus 1:13

3:8, 9 According to tradition, Jannes and Jambres were two of the magicians who had counterfeited Moses' miracles before Pharaoh (Exodus 7:11, 12). Paul explained that just as Moses had exposed and defeated them (Exodus 8:18, 19), God would overthrow the false teachers who were plaguing the Ephesian church.

• **3:9** We can hide our sin for a while, but eventually the truth will be revealed. Sooner or later, distraction, opposition, anger, or fatigue will wear us down, and our true hearts will be exposed. The trials of life will conspire against our efforts to maintain a religious front. We can't pick when and where we will be tested by adversity. Build your character carefully because it will come out under stress. Live each day as if your actions will one day be known to everyone. It is useless, in the middle of a test, to acknowledge that you should have prepared. Now is the time to change anything you wouldn't want revealed later.

3:11 In Lystra, Timothy's hometown, Paul had been stoned and left for dead (Acts 14:19); and this was only one incident among many. In 2 Corinthians 11:23-33 Paul summarized his lifetime of suffering for the sake of the Good News. Paul mentioned his suffering here to contrast his experience with that of the pleasure-seeking false teachers.

• **3:12** In this charge, Paul told Timothy that people who obey God and live for Christ will be persecuted. Don't be surprised when people misunderstand, criticize, and even try to hurt you because of what you believe and how you live. Don't give up. Continue to live as you know you should. God is the only one you need to please.

3:13 Don't expect false teachers and evil people to reform and change on their own. Left alone, they will go from bad to worse. If you have the opportunity, correct them so as to bring them back to faith in Christ. Fight for the truth, especially to protect younger Christians.

• **3:14** Besieged by false teachers and the inevitable pressures of a growing ministry, Timothy could easily have abandoned his faith or modified his doctrine. Once again Paul counseled Timothy to look to his past and to hold to the basic teachings about Jesus that are eternally true. Like Timothy, we are surrounded by false teachings. But we must not allow our society to distort or crowd out God's eternal truth. Spend time every day reflecting on the foundation of your Christian faith found in God's Word, the great truths that build up your life.

3:15 Timothy was one of the first second-generation Christians: He became a Christian, not because an evangelist preached a powerful sermon, but because his mother and grandmother had taught him the holy Scriptures when he was a small child (1:5). A parent's work is vitally important. At home and in church, we should realize that teaching small children is both an opportunity and a responsibility. Jesus wanted little children to come to him (Matthew 19:13-15). Like Timothy's mother and grandmother, Eunice and Lois, do your part in leading children to Christ.

3:15 For Timothy, the "holy Scriptures" were the books of the Old Testament. The Old Testament is important because it points to Jesus Christ. At the same time, faith in Christ makes the whole Bible intelligible.

3:16 The Bible is not a collection of stories, fables, myths, or merely human ideas about God. It is not a human book. Through the Holy Spirit, God revealed his person and plan to certain believers, who wrote down his message for his people (2 Peter 1:20, 21). This process is known as *inspiration*. The writers wrote from their own personal, historical, and cultural contexts. Although they used their own minds, talents, language, and style, they wrote what God wanted them to write. Scripture is completely trustworthy because God was in control of its writing. Its words are entirely authoritative for our faith and life. The Bible is "God-breathed." Read it, and use its teachings to guide your conduct.

3:16, 17 The whole Bible is God's inspired Word. Because it is inspired and trustworthy, we should *read* it and *apply* it to our life. The Bible is our standard for testing everything else that claims to be true. It is our safeguard against false teaching and our source of guidance for how we should live. It is our only source of knowledge about how we can be saved. God wants to show you what is true and equip you to live for him. How much time do you spend in God's Word? Read it regularly to discover God's truth and to become confident in your life and faith. Develop a plan for reading the whole Bible, not just the familiar passages.

3:17 In our zeal for the *truth* of Scripture, we must never forget its *purpose*—to equip us to do good. We should not study God's Word simply to increase our knowledge or to prepare us to win arguments. We should study the Bible so that we will know how to do Christ's work in the world. Our knowledge of God's Word is not useful unless it strengthens our faith and leads us to do good.

4:1, 2 It was important for Timothy to preach the Good News so that the Christian faith could spread throughout the world. We believe in Christ today because people like Timothy were faithful to their mission. It is still vitally important for believers to spread

4:3
2 Tim 3:1-2

4:4
1 Tim 1:4

4:5
2 Tim 1:8

4:7
1 Cor 9:24-27
Phil 3:12-14
1 Tim 6:12

4:8
1 Cor 9:25
Phil 3:14
Col 1:5
Rev 2:10

³For a time is coming when people will no longer listen to sound and wholesome teaching. They will follow their own desires and will look for teachers who will tell them whatever their itching ears want to hear. ⁴They will reject the truth and chase after myths.

⁵But you should keep a clear mind in every situation. Don't be afraid of suffering for the Lord. Work at telling others the Good News, and fully carry out the ministry God has given you.

⁶As for me, my life has already been poured out as an offering to God. The time of my death is near. ⁷I have fought the good fight, I have finished the race, and I have remained faithful. ⁸And now the prize awaits me—the crown of righteousness, which the Lord, the righteous Judge, will give me on the day of his return. And the prize is not just for me but for all who eagerly look forward to his appearing.

Paul's Final Words

4:11
Col 4:10, 14
Phlm 1:24

⁹Timothy, please come as soon as you can. ¹⁰Demas has deserted me because he loves the things of this life and has gone to Thessalonica. Crescens has gone to Galatia, and Titus has gone to Dalmatia. ¹¹Only Luke is with me. Bring Mark with you when you come, for he will

---

the Good News. Half the people who have ever lived are alive today, and most of them do not know Christ. He is coming soon, and he wants to find his faithful believers ready for him. It may be inconvenient to take a stand for Christ or to tell others about his love, but preaching the Word of God is the most important responsibility the church and its members have been given. Be prepared for, courageous in, and sensitive to God-given opportunities to tell the Good News.

• **4:2** We should always be ready to serve God in any situation, whether or not it is convenient. Be sensitive to the opportunities God gives you.

4:2 Paul told Timothy to "correct, rebuke, and encourage." It is difficult to accept correction, to be told we have to change. But no matter how much the truth hurts, we must be willing to listen to it so we can more fully obey God.

4:3-5 Many speakers, teachers, and writers talk about the pursuit of knowledge. But often they don't want knowledge; they want power. Such people won't listen to "sound and wholesome teaching." Instead, they "reject the truth and chase after myths." You can see this everywhere—from liberal churches to university campuses. People claiming to have a bit more enlightenment than what the dusty Bible has to say; people claiming to improve on God's words. Such people have several things in common: (1) *They do not tolerate the truth.* They have no interest or respect for absolute truth or any standard for judgment. (2) *They reject truth for sensationalism.* They want truth that fits their situation and makes sense for them. What they feel, what works for them, what seems compelling—that is their truth and they claim an absolute right to it. No one should even attempt to tell them differently. (3) *They gather viewpoints to suit their selfish desires.* Although they profess objectivity, their only defense for their viewpoints is that those viewpoints suit their desires.

Such teachers have a following because they are telling people "whatever their itching ears want to hear." These people are following myths. Be careful. False teaching can be found in many places—even inside the doors of some churches. Like Timothy, you must "keep a clear mind in every situation" and seek God's Word for the truth.

• **4:5** To keep cool when you are jarred and jolted by people or circumstances, don't react quickly. In any work of ministry that you undertake, keeping a clear mind in every situation makes you morally alert to temptation, resistant to pressure, and vigilant when facing heavy responsibility.

• **4:6-8** As he neared the end of his life, Paul could confidently say that he had been faithful to his call. Thus, he faced death calmly, knowing that he would be rewarded by Christ. Is your life preparing you for death? Do you share Paul's confident expectation of meeting Christ? The good news is that the heavenly reward is not just for giants of the faith like Paul, but for all who are eagerly looking forward to Christ's second coming. Paul gave these words

to encourage Timothy and us, so that no matter how difficult the fight seems, we can keep fighting. When we are with Jesus Christ, we will discover that it was all worth it.

4:8 In Roman athletic games, a laurel wreath would be given to each winner. A symbol of triumph and honor, it was the most coveted prize in ancient Rome. This is probably what Paul was referring to when he spoke of a "crown." But his would be a crown of righteousness. See 2 Corinthians 5:10 and the note on Matthew 19:27 for more on the rewards awaiting us for our faith and deeds. Although Paul would not receive an earthly reward, he would be rewarded in heaven. Whatever we may face—discouragement, persecution, or death—we know we will receive reward with Christ in heaven.

4:9, 10 Paul was virtually alone and probably lonely. No one had come to his trial to speak in his defense (4:16), and Demas had left the faith (4:10). Crescens and Titus had left, but not for the same reasons as Demas. Paul did not criticize or condemn them. Demas had been one of Paul's coworkers (Colossians 4:14; Philemon 1:24), but he had deserted Paul because he loved "the things of this life." In other words, Demas loved worldly values and worldly pleasures. There are two ways to love the world. God loves the world as he created it and as it could be if it were rescued from evil. Others, like Demas, love the world as it is, sin and all. Do you love the world as it could be if justice were done, the hungry were fed, and people loved one another? Or do you love what the world has to offer—wealth, power, pleasure—even if gaining it means hurting people and neglecting the work God has given you to do?

4:11, 12 Mentioning Demas reminded Paul of more faithful coworkers. Luke had traveled much with Paul, writing both the Gospel of Luke and the book of Acts (much of which is a firsthand account). Tychicus, one of his most trusted companions (Acts 20:4; Ephesians 6:21; Colossians 4:7; Titus 3:12), had already left for Ephesus.

That Paul requested for Timothy to bring Mark might give us pause. Mark had left Paul and Barnabas on the first missionary journey, and this had greatly upset Paul (Acts 13:13; 15:36-41), causing a rift between Paul and Barnabas that was so severe that they parted company. Somewhere along the line, Paul had given Mark a second chance, and Mark had proven to be a worthy helper. We don't have all the details in Mark's changed life or Paul's change of heart, but Paul realized that people can change.

There's a lesson in these few words. We should allow people to grow up and not hold them back from ministry or leadership for faults in the past that have now been corrected. When we encourage someone and open our minds to the possibility that he or she has changed and matured, we may be salvaging a significant ministry. Mark went on not only to be Paul's good friend and a trusted Christian leader (Colossians 4:10; Philemon 1:24), but he also wrote the Gospel of Mark.

be helpful to me in my ministry. ¹²I sent Tychicus to Ephesus. ¹³When you come, be sure to bring the coat I left with Carpus at Troas. Also bring my books, and especially my papers.*

¹⁴Alexander the coppersmith did me much harm, but the Lord will judge him for what he has done. ¹⁵Be careful of him, for he fought against everything we said.

¹⁶The first time I was brought before the judge, no one came with me. Everyone abandoned me. May it not be counted against them. ¹⁷But the Lord stood with me and gave me strength so that I might preach the Good News in its entirety for all the Gentiles to hear. And he rescued me from certain death.* ¹⁸Yes, and the Lord will deliver me from every evil attack and will bring me safely into his heavenly Kingdom. All glory to God forever and ever! Amen.

Paul's Final Greetings

¹⁹Give my greetings to Priscilla and Aquila and those living in the household of Onesiphorus. ²⁰Erastus stayed at Corinth, and I left Trophimus sick at Miletus.

²¹Do your best to get here before winter. Eubulus sends you greetings, and so do Pudens, Linus, Claudia, and all the brothers and sisters.*

²²May the Lord be with your spirit. And may his grace be with all of you.

4:13 Greek *especially the parchments.* 4:17 Greek *from the mouth of a lion.* 4:21 Greek *brothers.*

4:12
Acts 20:4
Eph 6:21-22
Col 4:7-8

4:14
1 Tim 1:20

4:17
Ps 22:21
Dan 6:22
Acts 9:15

4:18
Ps 121:7
Rom 11:36

4:19
Acts 18:2
2 Tim 1:16

4:20
Acts 19:22; 20:4
Rom 16:23

4:13 Paul's arrest probably had occurred so suddenly that he had not been allowed to return home to gather his personal belongings. Because he was a prisoner in a damp and chilly dungeon, Paul asked Timothy to bring him his coat. Even more than the coat, Paul wanted his papers (or parchments). These may have included parts of the Old Testament, the Gospels, copies of his own letters, or other important documents.

4:14, 15 Alexander may have been a witness against Paul at his trial. He may have been the Alexander mentioned in 1 Timothy 1:20.

4:17 With his mentor in prison and his church in turmoil, Timothy was probably not feeling very brave. Paul may have been subtly telling Timothy that the Lord had called Timothy to preach and would give him the courage to continue to do so. God always gives us the strength to do what he has commanded. This strength may not be evident, however, until we step out in faith and actually begin doing the task.

● **4:18** Here Paul was affirming his belief in eternal life after death. Paul knew the end was near, and he was ready for it. Paul was confident in God's power even as he faced death. Anyone facing a life-and-death struggle can be comforted knowing that God will bring each believer safely through death to his heavenly Kingdom.

4:19, 20 Priscilla and Aquila were fellow Christian leaders with whom Paul had lived and worked (Acts 18:2, 3). Onesiphorus visited and encouraged Paul in jail. Erastus was one of Paul's

trusted companions (Acts 19:22), as was Trophimus (Acts 20:4; 21:29).

4:19-22 Paul ended the final chapter in his book and in his life by greeting those who were closest to him. Although Paul had spent most of his life traveling, he had developed close and lasting friendships. Too often we rush through our days, barely touching anyone's life. Do you have a Paul—a mentor or teacher who provides leadership, accountability, and encouragement? Do you have a Priscilla or Aquila—a coworker or peer who prays with you in times of stress, loves you, and supports you? Do you have a Timothy—a younger leader whom you are helping, encouraging, and discipling? Like Paul, we should take time to weave our lives into others' through close personal relationships.

● **4:22** As Paul reached the end of his life, he could look back and know he had been faithful to God's call. Now it was time to pass the torch to the next generation, preparing leaders to take his place so that the world would continue to hear the life-changing message of Jesus Christ. Timothy was Paul's living legacy, a product of Paul's faithful teaching, discipleship, and example. Because of Paul's work with many believers, including Timothy, the world is filled with believers today who are also carrying on the work. What legacy will you leave behind? Whom are you training to carry on your work? It is our responsibility to do all we can to keep God's Good News alive for the next generation.

TITUS

TITUS

THE VACUUM produced when a strong leader departs can devastate a movement, organization, or institution. Having been dependent on his or her skill, style, and personality, associates and subordinates flounder or vie for control. Soon efficiency and vitality are lost, and decline and demise follow. Often this pattern is repeated in churches. A great speaker or teacher gathers a following, and soon a church is flourishing. It is alive, vital, and effective. Lives are being changed and people led into the Kingdom. But when this person leaves or dies, with him or her goes the drive and the heart of the organization.

People flocked to hear Paul's teaching. Educated, articulate, motivated, and filled with the Holy Spirit, this man of God faithfully proclaimed the Good News throughout the Roman Empire; lives were changed and churches begun. But Paul knew that the church must be built on Christ, not on a person. And he knew that eventually he would not be there to build, encourage, discipline, and teach. So he trained young pastors to assume leadership in the churches after he was gone. Paul urged them to center their lives and preaching on the Word of God (2 Timothy 3:16, 17) and to train others to carry on the ministry (2 Timothy 2:2).

Titus was a Greek believer. Taught and nurtured by Paul, he stood before the leaders of the church in Jerusalem as a living example of what Christ was doing among the Gentiles (Galatians 2:1–3). Like Timothy, he was one of Paul's trusted traveling companions and closest friends. Later he became Paul's special ambassador (2 Corinthians 7:5–16) and eventually the overseer of the churches on Crete (Titus 1:5). Slowly and carefully, Paul developed Titus into a mature Christian and a responsible leader. The letter to Titus was a step in this discipleship process. As with Timothy, Paul told Titus how to organize and lead the churches.

Paul begins his letter with a longer than usual greeting and introduction, outlining the leadership progression: Paul's ministry (1:1–3), Titus's responsibilities (1:4, 5), and those leaders whom Titus would appoint and train (1:5). Paul then lists pastoral qualifications (1:6–9) and contrasts faithful elders with the false leaders and teachers (1:10–16).

Next, Paul emphasizes the importance of good deeds in the life of the Christian, telling Titus how to relate to the various age groups in the church (2:2–6). He urges Titus to be a good example of a mature believer (2:7, 8) and to teach with courage and conviction (2:9–15). He then discusses the general responsibilities of Christians in society: Titus should remind the people of these (3:1–8), and he should avoid divisive arguments (3:9–11). Paul concludes with a few matters of itinerary and personal greetings (3:12–15).

Paul's letter to Titus is brief, but it is an important link in the discipleship process, helping a young man grow into leadership in the church. As you read this pastoral letter, you will gain insight into the organization and life of the early church, and you will find principles for structuring contemporary churches. But you should also see how to be a responsible Christian leader. Read the letter to Titus and determine, like Paul, to train men and women to lead and teach others.

VITAL STATISTICS

PURPOSE:
To advise Titus in his responsibility of supervising the churches on the island of Crete

AUTHOR:
Paul

ORIGINAL AUDIENCE:
Titus, a Greek, probably converted to Christ through Paul's ministry (he had become Paul's special representative to the island of Crete)

DATE WRITTEN:
Approximately A.D. 64, around the same time 1 Timothy was written; probably from Macedonia when Paul traveled between his Roman imprisonments

SETTING:
Paul sent Titus to organize and oversee the churches on Crete. This letter tells Titus how to do this job.

KEY VERSE:
"I left you on the island of Crete so you could complete our work there and appoint elders in each town as I instructed you" (1:5).

KEY PEOPLE:
Paul, Titus

KEY PLACES:
Crete, Nicopolis

SPECIAL FEATURES:
Titus is very similar to 1 Timothy with its instructions to church leaders.

THE BLUEPRINT

1. Leadership in the church (1:1–16)
2. Right living in the church (2:1–15)
3. Right living in society (3:1–15)

Paul calls for church order and right living on an island known for laziness, gluttony, lying, and evil. The Christians are to be self-disciplined as individuals, and they must be orderly as people who form one body, the church. We need to obey this message in our day when discipline is not respected or rewarded by our society. Although others may not appreciate our efforts, we must live upright lives, obey the government, and control our speech. We should live together peacefully in the church and be living examples of our faith to contemporary society.

MEGATHEMES

THEME	EXPLANATION	IMPORTANCE
A Good Life	The Good News of salvation is that we can't be saved by living a good life; we are saved only by faith in Jesus Christ. But the gospel transforms people's lives, so that they eventually perform good deeds. Our service won't save us, but we are saved to serve.	A good life is a witness to the gospel's power. As Christians, we must have commitment and discipline to serve. Are you putting your faith into action by serving others?
Character	Titus's responsibility in Crete was to appoint elders to maintain proper organization and discipline, so Paul listed the qualities needed for the eldership. Their conduct in their homes revealed their fitness for service in the church.	It's not enough to be educated or to have a loyal following to be Christ's kind of leader. You must have self-control, spiritual and moral fitness, and Christian character. Who you are is just as important as what you can do.
Church Relationships	Church teaching must relate to various groups. Older Christians were to teach and to be examples to younger men and women. People of every age and group have a lesson to learn and a role to play.	Right living and right relationships go along with right doctrine. Treat relationships with other believers as an outgrowth of your faith.
Citizenship	Christians must be good citizens in society, not just in church. Believers must obey the government and work honestly.	How you fulfill your civic duties is a witness to the watching world. Your community life should reflect Christ's love as much as your church life does.

1. Leadership in the church

Greetings from Paul

1 This letter is from Paul, a slave of God and an apostle of Jesus Christ. I have been sent to proclaim faith to* those God has chosen and to teach them to know the truth that shows them how to live godly lives. 2 This truth gives them confidence that they have eternal life, which God—who does not lie—promised them before the world began. 3 And now at just the right time he has revealed this message, which we announce to everyone. It is by the command of God our Savior that I have been entrusted with this work for him.

1:1
1 Tim 2:4

1:2
2 Tim 1:1, 9
Titus 3:7

1:3
1 Tim 1:1, 11
Titus 2:10

1:1 Or *to strengthen the faith of.*

• **1:1** Paul wrote this letter between his first and second imprisonments in Rome (before he wrote 2 Timothy) to guide Titus in working with the churches on the island of Crete. Paul had visited Crete with Titus and had left him there to minister (1:5). Crete had a strong pagan influence because this small island may have been a training center for Roman soldiers. Therefore, the church in Crete needed strong Christian leadership.

1:1 Paul calls himself "a slave of God"—that is, one who was committed to obeying God. This obedience led Paul to spend his life telling others about Christ. He also calls himself "an apostle." Even though Paul was not one of the original 12, he was specially called by God to bring the Good News to the Gentiles (see Acts 9:1-16 for an account of his call). The word *apostle* means "messenger or missionary." "Those God has chosen" refers to God's choice of his people, the church. For more information on Paul, see his Profile in Acts 9, p. 1837.

1:1 In one short phrase, Paul gives insight into his reason for living. The process begins with the proclamation of *faith*, continues with *knowledge* of the truth, which is then shown by people living *godly lives*. Paul wanted men and women to be mature in

Jesus Christ. This was his ultimate objective by which he evaluated all he did.

How would your church evaluate its ultimate objectives? What specific goals, ministries, and service opportunities bring believers to faith, spiritual maturity, and godly living? Do established members reflect good Christian conduct and desire for Christian service?

How would you describe your purpose in life? To what are you devoted? Are you willing to share your faith, teach the truth, and live a godly life for all to see?

• **1:2** Apparently lying was commonplace in Crete (1:12). Paul made it clear at the start that God does not lie. The foundation of our faith is trust in God's character. Because God *is* truth, he is the *source* of all truth, and he cannot lie. Believing in him leads to living a God-honoring lifestyle (1:1). The eternal life that God has promised will be ours because he keeps his promises. Build your faith on the foundation of a trustworthy God who never lies.

1:3 God is called "our Savior," as is Christ Jesus (1:4). "God" here refers to the Father. Jesus did the work of salvation by dying for our sins, and, therefore, he is our Savior. God planned the

1:4
2 Cor 2:13
2 Tim 4:10

⁴I am writing to Titus, my true son in the faith that we share.

May God the Father and Christ Jesus our Savior give you grace and peace.

Titus's Work in Crete

1:5
Acts 14:23

⁵I left you on the island of Crete so you could complete our work there and appoint elders

1:6-9
//1 Tim 3:2-7
2 Tim 2:24-26

in each town as I instructed you. ⁶An elder must live a blameless life. He must be faithful to his wife,* and his children must be believers who don't have a reputation for being wild or rebellious. ⁷An elder* is a manager of God's household, so he must live a blameless

1:7
1 Cor 4:1

life. He must not be arrogant or quick-tempered; he must not be a heavy drinker,* violent, or dishonest with money.

⁸Rather, he must enjoy having guests in his home, and he must love what is good. He must

1:6 Or *must have only one wife,* or *must be married only once;* Greek reads *must be the husband of one wife.*
1:7a Or *An overseer,* or *A bishop.* **1:7b** Greek *must not drink too much wine.*

TITUS GOES TO CRETE
Tradition says that after Paul was released from prison in Rome (before his second and final Roman imprisonment), he and Titus traveled together for a while. They stopped in Crete, and when it was time for Paul to go, he left Titus behind to help the churches there.

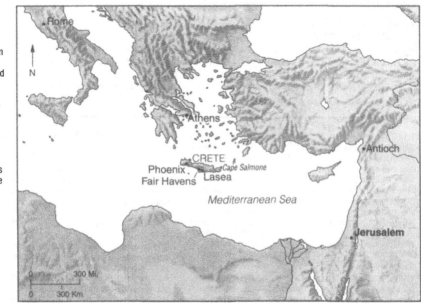

work of salvation, and he forgives our sins. Both the Father and the Son acted to save us from our sins.

1:4 Titus, a Greek, was one of Paul's most trusted and dependable coworkers. Paul had sent Titus to Corinth on several special missions to help the church in its troubles (2 Corinthians 7–8). Paul and Titus also had traveled together to Jerusalem (Galatians 2:3) and Crete (1:5). Paul left Titus in Crete to lead the new churches that were springing up on the island. Titus is last mentioned by Paul in 2 Timothy 4:10, Paul's final recorded letter. Titus had leadership ability, so Paul gave him leadership responsibility, urging him to use his abilities well.

• **1:5** Crete, a small island in the Mediterranean Sea, had a large population of Jews. The churches there were probably founded by Cretan Jews who had been in Jerusalem at Pentecost (Acts 2:11) more than 30 years before Paul wrote this letter. The work that needed completion refers to establishing correct teaching and appointing elders in every town. Paul had appointed elders in various churches during his journeys (Acts 14:23). He could not stay in each church, but he knew that these new churches needed strong spiritual leadership. The men chosen were to lead the churches by teaching sound doctrine, helping believers mature spiritually, and equipping them to live for Jesus Christ despite opposition.

• **1:5-9** Paul briefly describes some qualifications that the elders should have. Paul had given Timothy a similar set of instructions for the church in Ephesus (see 1 Timothy 3:1-7; 5:22). Notice that most of the qualifications involve character, not knowledge or skill. A person's lifestyle and relationships provide a window into his or her character. Consider these qualifications as you evaluate a person for a position of leadership in your church. It is important to have leaders who can effectively preach God's Word; it is even more important to have those who can live out God's Word and be examples for others to follow.

1:8 One qualification for an elder was that he must "enjoy having guests in his home." Christian leaders must be known for their hospitality. In the early days of Christianity, traveling evangelists and teachers were helped by Christians who housed and fed them. We would benefit from inviting people to eat with us—visitors, fellow church members, young people, those in need. Giving hospitality is very important today because so many people struggle with loneliness. In our self-centered society, we can show that we care by being hospitable. Christians were not to entertain false teachers (2 John 1:10), but this prohibition did not apply to non-Christians in general. God wants us to be generous, courteous, and hospitable with non-Christians; through our friendship, some may be won to Christ.

live wisely and be just. He must live a devout and disciplined life. 9He must have a strong belief in the trustworthy message he was taught; then he will be able to encourage others with wholesome teaching and show those who oppose it where they are wrong.

10For there are many rebellious people who engage in useless talk and deceive others. This is especially true of those who insist on circumcision for salvation. 11They must be silenced, because they are turning whole families away from the truth by their false teaching. And they do it only for money. 12Even one of their own men, a prophet from Crete, has said about them, "The people of Crete are all liars, cruel animals, and lazy gluttons."* 13This is true. So reprimand them sternly to make them strong in the faith. 14They must stop listening to Jewish myths and the commands of people who have turned away from the truth.

15Everything is pure to those whose hearts are pure. But nothing is pure to those who are corrupt and unbelieving, because their minds and consciences are corrupted. 16Such people claim they know God, but they deny him by the way they live. They are detestable and disobedient, worthless for doing anything good.

2. Right living in the church
Promote Right Teaching

2 As for you, Titus, promote the kind of living that reflects wholesome teaching. 2Teach the older men to exercise self-control, to be worthy of respect, and to live wisely. They must have sound faith and be filled with love and patience.

3Similarly, teach the older women to live in a way that honors God. They must not slander

1:9
1 Tim 1:10
2 Tim 4:3
Titus 2:1
1:10
1 Tim 1:6
1:11
1 Tim 5:13
1:13
1 Tim 5:20
1:14
Col 2:22
1 Tim 1:4; 4:7
2 Tim 4:4
1:15
Matt 15:10-11
Rom 14:14-20
1:16
1 Jn 1:6; 2:4
2:1
1 Tim 1:10
Titus 1:9
2:3
1 Tim 3:8, 11

1:12 This quotation is from Epimenides of Knossos.

1:10 "Those who insist on circumcision for salvation" were the Judaizers, Jews who taught that the Gentiles had to obey all the Jewish laws before they could become Christians. This regulation confused new Christians and caused problems in many churches where Paul had preached the Good News. Paul wrote letters to several churches to help them understand that Gentile believers did not have to become Jews first in order to be Christians; God accepts anyone who comes to him in faith (see Romans 1:17; Galatians 3:2-7). Although the Jerusalem council had dealt with this issue (see Acts 15), devout Jews who refused to believe in Jesus still tried to cause problems in the Christian churches. Church leaders must be alert and take action on anything that divides Christians.

1:10-14 Paul warns Titus to be on the lookout for people who teach wrong doctrines and lead others into error. Some false teachers are simply confused: They speak their misguided opinions without checking them against the Bible. Others have evil motives: They pretend to be Christians only because they can get more money, additional business, or a feeling of power from being a leader in the church. Jesus and the apostles repeatedly warned against false teachers (see Mark 13:22; Acts 20:29; 2 Thessalonians 2:3-12; 2 Peter 3:3-7) because their teachings attack the foundations of truth and integrity upon which the Christian faith is built. You can recognize false teachers because they will (1) focus more attention on themselves than on Christ, (2) ask you to do something that will compromise or dilute your faith, (3) de-emphasize the divine nature of Christ or the inspiration of the Bible, or (4) urge believers to make decisions based more on human judgment than on prayer and biblical guidelines.

1:12 Paul is quoting a line from a poem by Epimenides, a poet and philosopher who had lived in Crete 600 years earlier. Some Cretans had a bad reputation and were known for lying. Paul used this familiar phrase to make the point that Titus's ministry and leadership were very much needed.

• **1:15** Some people see good all around them, while others see nothing but evil. What is the difference? Our souls become filters through which we perceive goodness or evil. The pure (those who have Christ in control of their lives) learn to see goodness and purity even in this evil world. But corrupt and unbelieving people find evil in everything because their evil minds and hearts color even the good they see and hear. Whatever you choose to fill your mind with will affect the way you think and act. Turn your

thoughts to God and his Word, and you will discover more and more goodness, even in this evil world. A mind filled with good has little room for what is evil (see Philippians 4:8).

1:16 Many people claim to know God. How can we know if they really do? We will not know for certain in this life, but a glance at their lifestyles will quickly tell us what they value and whether they have ordered their lives around Kingdom priorities. Our conduct speaks volumes about what we believe (see 1 John 2:4-6). What do people know about God and about your faith by watching your life?

2:1 Notice the emphasis on "wholesome teaching" in Paul's instructions to Titus. This is the *content* of our faith. But how can you recognize wholesome teaching? When a teaching is sound, it combines correct knowledge and understanding with consistent practice. It must be found in the Bible, keep Jesus Christ central, result in consistently good behavior and actions, and promote spiritual health in ourselves and others.

Believers must be grounded in the truths of the Bible so they won't be swayed by the powerful oratory of false teachers, the possible devastation of tragic circumstances, or the pull of emotions. Those responsible for preaching and teaching must challenge people to understand sound doctrine. Learn the Bible, study theology, apply biblical principles, and *live* what you learn.

• **2:2-8** Having people of all ages in the church makes it strong, but it also brings potential for problems. Paul gave Titus counsel on how to help various groups of people. The older people should teach the younger by words *and* by example. This is how values are passed on from generation to generation. Does your church carry out this basic function?

• **2:2, 5** Self-control is an important aspect of living the Christian life. The Christian community, then and now, is made up of people from differing backgrounds and viewpoints, making conflict inevitable. We live in a pagan and often hostile world. To stay above reproach, believers need wisdom and discernment to be discreet and to master their wills, tongues, and passions so that Christ is not dishonored. How is your self-control?

2:3-5 Women who were new Christians were to learn how to have harmony in the homes by watching older women who had been Christians for some time. We have the same need today. Young wives and mothers should learn to live in a Christian manner—loving their husbands and caring for their children—through observing exemplary women of God. If you are of an age or in

2:5
Eph 5:22
1 Tim 5:14

2:7
1 Tim 4:12
1 Pet 5:3

2:8
1 Pet 2:12

2:9
Eph 6:5

2:11
1 Tim 2:4
2 Tim 1:10

2:13
John 1:1; 20:28
Rom 9:5
1 Cor 1:7
Phil 3:20
2 Pet 1:1
1 Jn 5:20

2:14
Eph 2:10
1 Pet 2:9
1 Jn 1:7

2:15
1 Tim 4:12

3:1
Rom 13:1
1 Pet 2:13

3:2
Eph 4:31

others or be heavy drinkers.* Instead, they should teach others what is good. ⁴These older women must train the younger women to love their husbands and their children, ⁵to live wisely and be pure, to work in their homes,* to do good, and to be submissive to their husbands. Then they will not bring shame on the word of God.

⁶In the same way, encourage the young men to live wisely. ⁷And you yourself must be an example to them by doing good works of every kind. Let everything you do reflect the integrity and seriousness of your teaching. ⁸Teach the truth so that your teaching can't be criticized. Then those who oppose us will be ashamed and have nothing bad to say about us.

⁹Slaves must always obey their masters and do their best to please them. They must not talk back ¹⁰or steal, but must show themselves to be entirely trustworthy and good. Then they will make the teaching about God our Savior attractive in every way.

¹¹For the grace of God has been revealed, bringing salvation to all people. ¹²And we are instructed to turn from godless living and sinful pleasures. We should live in this evil world with wisdom, righteousness, and devotion to God, ¹³while we look forward with hope to that wonderful day when the glory of our great God and Savior, Jesus Christ, will be revealed. ¹⁴He gave his life to free us from every kind of sin, to cleanse us, and to make us his very own people, totally committed to doing good deeds.

¹⁵You must teach these things and encourage the believers to do them. You have the authority to correct them when necessary, so don't let anyone disregard what you say.

3. Right living in society
Do What Is Good

3 Remind the believers to submit to the government and its officers. They should be obedient, always ready to do what is good. ²They must not slander anyone and must avoid quarreling. Instead, they should be gentle and show true humility to everyone.

2:3 Greek *be enslaved to much wine.*   **2:5** Some manuscripts read *to care for their homes.*

---

a position where people look up to you, make sure that your example is motivating younger believers to live in a way that honors God.

• **2:6** This advice given to young men was very important. In ancient Greek society, the role of the husband/father was not viewed as a nurturing role but merely as a functional one. Many young men today have been raised in families where fathers have neglected their responsibilities to their wives and children. Husbands and fathers who are good examples of Christian living are important role models for young men who need to *see* how it is done.

• **2:7, 8** Paul urges Titus to be a good example to those around him so that others might see Titus's good deeds and imitate him. Paul's life would give his words greater impact. If you want someone to act a certain way, be sure that you live that way yourself. Then you will earn the right to be heard, and your life will reinforce what you teach.

• **2:8** Paul counsels Titus to be above criticism in how he taught. This quality of integrity comes from careful Bible study and listening before speaking. This is especially important when teaching or confronting others about spiritual or moral issues. If we are impulsive, unreasonable, and confusing, we are likely to start arguments rather than to convince people of the truth.

• **2:9, 10** Slavery was common in Paul's day. Paul did not condemn slavery in any of his letters, but he advised slaves and masters to be loving and responsible in their conduct (see also Ephesians 6:5-9). The standards set by Paul can help any employee/employer relationship. Employees should always do their best work and be trustworthy, not just when the employer is watching. Businesses lose millions of dollars a year to employee theft and time-wasting. If all Christian employees would follow Paul's advice at work, what a transformation it would make!

2:12, 13 Paul brings out two aspects of Christian living that must be stressed today. "We should live in this evil world . . . while we look forward with hope." Both aspects of *living* and *looking forward* are essential to our Christian sanity in this present evil age. The living is made bearable because we live for God—seeking to build his Kingdom with whatever gifts he has given us. And it is that very Kingdom to which we are looking forward. As we live and look

forward, we anticipate three great benefits of Christ's return: (1) Christ's personal presence—we look forward to being with him. (2) Redemption from our sinful nature—we long for the end of the battle with sin and our perfection in Christ. (3) Restoration of creation—we anticipate the complete rule of grace when the image of God will be fully realized in people and when the created order will be restored.

2:14 Christ's freeing us from sin opens the way for him to "cleanse" us. He freed us from sin (redeemed us) by purchasing our release from the captivity of sin with a ransom (see Mark 10:45 for more on Christ as our ransom). We are not only free from the sentence of death for our sin, but we are also purified from sin's influence as we grow in Christ.

• **2:15** Paul tells Titus to teach the Scriptures as well as to live them. We must also teach, encourage, and correct others, when necessary. We can easily feel afraid when others are older, more influential in the community, or wealthier. Like Titus, we should not let ourselves be threatened when we are trying to minister to others or provide leadership in the church.

• **3:1** As Christians, our first allegiance is to Jesus as Lord, but we must obey our government and its leaders as well. Christians are not above the law. Obeying the civil law is only the beginning of our Christian responsibility; we must do what we can to be good citizens. (See Acts 5:29 and Romans 13:1ff for more on the Christian's attitude toward government.)

3:2 How does one "show true humility"? Humility is a very elusive character trait, yet the Bible regards it as a highly important quality. Jesus referred to himself as "humble and gentle at heart" (Matthew 11:29). In Romans 12:3, Paul wrote the clearest definition of humility apart from Jesus' own example: "Don't think you are better than you really are. Be honest in your evaluation of yourselves, measuring yourselves by the faith God has given us."

Humility, then, boils down to having an honest estimate of ourselves before God. We show false humility when we project negative worth on our abilities and efforts. We show pride when we inflate the value of our efforts or look down on others. True humility seeks to view our character and accomplishments honestly. Recognizing that we have succeeded in an effort need not be pride.

3Once we, too, were foolish and disobedient. We were misled and became slaves to many lusts and pleasures. Our lives were full of evil and envy, and we hated each other. 4But—"When God our Savior revealed his kindness and love, 5he saved us, not because of the righteous things we had done, but because of his mercy. He washed away our sins, giving us a new birth and new life through the Holy Spirit.* 6He generously poured out the Spirit upon us through Jesus Christ our Savior. 7Because of his grace he declared us righteous and gave us confidence that we will inherit eternal life." 8This is a trustworthy saying, and I want you to insist on these teachings so that all who trust in God will devote themselves to doing good. These teachings are good and beneficial for everyone.

9Do not get involved in foolish discussions about spiritual pedigrees* or in quarrels and fights about obedience to Jewish laws. These things are useless and a waste of time. 10If people are causing divisions among you, give a first and second warning. After that, have nothing more to do with them. 11For people like that have turned away from the truth, and their own sins condemn them.

3:3
1 Cor 6:11
Eph 5:8

3:5
John 3:5
Eph 2:4, 8
1 Pet 1:3

3:6
Joel 2:28
Rom 5:5

3:7
Rom 3:24

3:8
Titus 2:14; 3:14

3:9
2 Tim 2:14, 16, 23

3:10
Matt 18:15-17
Rom 16:17

Paul's Final Remarks and Greetings

12I am planning to send either Artemas or Tychicus to you. As soon as one of them arrives, do your best to meet me at Nicopolis, for I have decided to stay there for the winter. 13Do everything you can to help Zenas the lawyer and Apollos with their trip. See that they are given everything they need. 14Our people must learn to do good by meeting the urgent needs of others; then they will not be unproductive.

15Everybody here sends greetings. Please give my greetings to the believers—all who love us.

May God's grace be with you all.

3:12
Acts 20:4
Eph 6:21-22
2 Tim 4:9, 21

3:13
Acts 18:24

3:14
Eph 4:28
Titus 2:14; 3:8

3:15
Col 4:18

3:5 Greek *He saved us through the washing of regeneration and renewing of the Holy Spirit.* **3:9** Or *spiritual genealogies.*

• **3:3** Following a life of pleasure and giving in to every sensual desire leads to slavery. Many think freedom consists of doing anything they want. But this path leads to a slavish addiction to sensual gratification. A person is no longer free but is a slave to what his or her body dictates (2 Peter 2:19). Christ frees us from the desires and control of sin. Have you been released?

• **3:4-8** Paul summarizes what Christ does for us when he saves us. We move from a life full of sin to one where we are led by God's Holy Spirit. *All* our sins, not merely some, are washed away. Washing refers to the water of baptism, which is a sign of salvation. In becoming a Christian, the believer acknowledges Christ as Lord and recognizes Christ's saving work. We gain eternal life with *all* its treasures. We have a new life through the Holy Spirit, and he continually renews our hearts. None of this occurs because we earned or deserved it; it is all God's gift.

• **3:4-6** All three persons of the Trinity are mentioned in these verses because all three participate in the work of salvation. Based upon the redemptive work of his Son, the Father forgives us and sends the Holy Spirit to wash away our sins and continually renew us.

3:8 In this chapter, Paul stressed that believers must devote themselves to doing good. Paul understood good works as faithful service, acts of charity, and involvement in civil affairs. While good works can't save us or even increase God's love for us, they are true indications of our faith and love for Christ. Paul did not make this aspect of discipleship optional. Service to others is a requirement. Everyone who is a Christian should be involved. Does your church encourage everyone's involvement and service? What can your church do to help every member identify the good works he or she should be doing?

3:9 Paul warns Titus, as he warned Timothy, not to get involved in foolish and unprofitable arguments (2 Timothy 2:14). This does not mean we should refuse to study, discuss, and examine different interpretations of difficult Bible passages. Paul is warning against petty quarrels, not honest discussion that leads to wisdom. If foolish arguments develop, it is best to turn the discussion back to a helpful direction or politely excuse yourself.

3:9 The false teachers were basing their heresies on spiritual pedigrees and speculations about the Jewish laws (see 1 Timothy 1:3, 4). Similar to the methods used by false teachers in Ephesus and Colosse, they were building their case on genealogies of angels. We should avoid false teachers, not even bothering to get involved in their foolish discussions. Overreaction sometimes gives more attention to their points of view.

3:10, 11 A person must be warned when he or she is causing division that threatens the unity of the church. This should not be a heavy-handed action but a warning to correct the individual's divisive nature and restore him or her to fellowship. A person who refuses to be corrected should be put outside the fellowship. As Paul said, that person is self-condemned—he or she is sinning and knows it. (See also Matthew 18:15-18 and 2 Thessalonians 3:14, 15 for help in handling such problems in the church.)

3:12 The city of Nicopolis was on the western coast of Greece. Artemas or Tychicus would take over Titus's work on the island of Crete so Titus could meet Paul in Nicopolis. Tychicus was another of Paul's trusted companions (Acts 20:4; Ephesians 6:21; Colossians 4:7). Titus would have to leave soon because sea travel was dangerous in the winter months.

3:13 Apollos was a famous Christian preacher. A native of Alexandria in North Africa, he became a Christian in Ephesus and was trained by Aquila and Priscilla (Acts 18:24-28; 1 Corinthians 1:12).

3:15 The letters of Paul to Titus and Timothy are his last writings and mark the end of his life and ministry. These letters are rich treasures for us today because they give vital information for church leadership. They provide a strong model for elders, pastors, and other Christian leaders as they develop younger leaders to carry on the work, following Paul's example of preparing Timothy and Titus to carry on his ministry. For practical guidelines on church leadership and problem solving, carefully study the principles found in these letters.

STUDY QUESTIONS

Thirteen lessons for individual or group study

It's always exciting to get more than you expect. And that's what you'll find in this Bible study guide—much more than you expect. Our goal was to write thoughtful, practical, dependable, and application-oriented studies of God's word.

This study guide contains the complete text of the selected Bible book. The commentary is accurate, complete, and loaded with unique charts, maps, and profiles of Bible people.

With the Bible text, extensive notes and features, and questions to guide discussion, Life Application Bible Studies have everything you need in one place.

The lessons in this Bible study guide will work for large classes as well as small-group studies. To get everyone involved in your discussions, encourage participants to answer the questions before each meeting.

Each lesson is divided into five easy-to-lead sections. The section called "Reflect" introduces you and the members of your group to a specific area of life touched by the lesson. "Read" shows which chapters to read and which notes and other features to use. Additional questions help you understand the passage. "Realize" brings into focus the biblical principle to be learned with questions, a special insight, or both. "Respond" helps you make connections with your own situation and personal needs. The questions are designed to help you find areas in your life where you can apply the biblical truths. "Resolve" helps you map out action plans for that day.

Begin and end each lesson with prayer, asking for the Holy Spirit's guidance, direction, and wisdom.

Recommended time allotments for each section of a lesson are as follows:

Segment	60 minutes	90 minutes
Reflect on your life	*5 minutes*	*10 minutes*
Read the passage	*10 minutes*	*15 minutes*
Realize the principle	*15 minutes*	*20 minutes*
Respond to the message	*20 minutes*	*30 minutes*
Resolve to take action	*10 minutes*	*15 minutes*

All five sections work together to help a person learn the lessons, live out the principles, and obey the commands taught in the Bible.

Also, at the end of each lesson, there is a section entitled "More for studying other themes in this section." These questions will help you lead the group in studying other parts of each section not covered in depth by the main lesson.

But don't just listen to God's word. You must do what it says. Otherwise, you are only fooling yourselves. For if you listen to the word and don't obey, it is like glancing at your face in a mirror. You see yourself, walk away, and forget what you look like. But if you look carefully into the perfect law that sets you free, and if you do what it says and don't forget what you heard, then God will bless you for doing it (James 1:22-25).

LESSON 1
LEADERSHIP LETTERS
1 TIMOTHY INTRODUCTION

REFLECT
on your life

1 List three well-known leaders in each of these areas:

Government/Politics	Business	Sports/Entertainment	Religion
_____	_____	_____	_____
_____	_____	_____	_____
_____	_____	_____	_____

2 What qualities do you appreciate most in your leaders?

Honesty, Transparency, humility, Integrity, perseverance

READ
the passage

Read the two-page introduction to 1 Timothy, "Vital Statistics" from both the introduction to Titus and the introduction to 2 Timothy, and the following study notes in 1 Timothy:

❏ 1:1   ❏ 1:3, 4

3 Who was Timothy? Why did Paul write this letter to him?

Paul's son in Faith, Paul's protégé, a young minister
To help him, encourage & teach him

4 What does the term *pastoral letters* mean?

Letters written to pastors

5 What was happening in these churches that made preserving right teaching so important?

They were being deceived by false prophets

6 What are some of the advantages of studying these three books in a different order than that in which they appear in the Bible?

Chronilogical order can help makes things clearer

The New Testament books of 1 Timothy, 2 Timothy, and Titus are letters from Paul to two young pastors whom he sent to provide leadership for the churches in teaching. They were churches in crisis. The practical topics that Paul addressed in these personal letters are also helpful for church leaders today. Wholesome teaching, public worship, and selection of leaders remain central areas of concern for both new and established churches. The letters contain solutions to solving the leadership crisis faced by many churches today. Whether you currently are a leader in your church, aspire to leadership, or are a new believer, you can take these letters personally. No matter what your position in your church, you have an important part in resolving the leadership crisis.

7 How are you a leader in your church? How can a person be a leader even though all he or she does is help out?

By example

8 Paul told Timothy to uphold wholesome teaching and a godly lifestyle. How are we in danger of mishandling these assignments today?

Its easier to follow a worldly lifestyle
Its easy to put God on the back burner
By not reading & studying God's word

RESPOND
to the message

9 Paul wrote his first letter to Timothy to give him practical advice for the ministry. In what areas of ministry do you need practical advice at this time?

_____

_____

_____

10 Which is most difficult for you: knowing what to believe, understanding your role in the church, or knowing how to lead with compassion? Why?

Compassion cause sometimes I'm too practical

_____

_____

_____

11 Who has been a mentor for you in your spiritual growth and ministry? Who have you mentored? How did you learn what you know about serving in the local church?

Pastor Ron, Thomas', Nebeker's, Kenneda's
Sunday school, church mostly

_____

_____

_____

12 Think of a time when you were young, inexperienced, or afraid that others would look down on you. Who or what helped you find strength and courage to handle the situation?

_____

_____

_____

13 In which of your responsibilities at church or any other area of ministry do you feel inadequate or afraid? How is your situation similar to what Timothy and Titus were facing?

Deaconesses - calling people setting up meals

_____

_____

_____

14 If Paul were to write a personal letter to you at this point in your life, what areas of concern would you want him to address? What questions would you have for him?

Prayer, Study, Bible reading

15 What do you most need from a study of Timothy and Titus? In what areas of your life or ministry do you need wise advice at this time? List your personal goals for this study.

Growth, Knowledge

RESOLVE
to take action

A What was happening in Ephesus that worried Paul? Why did he send Timothy? What was Timothy's mission? What would Paul ask Timothy to do in your church?

MORE
for studying
other themes
in this section

B Why would public worship be an area that Paul might address in this letter? What concerns you about worship in churches today?

C Paul lists important qualities for leaders. Why are these qualities important for our leaders today? What are some of the common mistakes we make in selecting leaders for our churches?

D For what groups of believers do these books contain important advice? To which of these groups do you belong?

E What do these books tell us about the importance of personal relationships between leaders and followers? What impresses you about the relationship between Timothy and Paul?

F At what point in the book of Acts was each of these letters most likely written?

G Who does the work of overseeing and strengthening the churches today? Where can a church in trouble turn for help?

LESSON 2
BUILDING ON A FIRM FOUNDATION
1 TIMOTHY 1:1-20

REFLECT
on your life

1 Why is a solid foundation important for a building? In what other contexts is it important to build a solid foundation?

_____

_____

_____

2 Why is a solid foundation important for our faith?

_____

_____

_____

READ
the passage

Read 1 Timothy 1:1-20 and the following notes:

❏ 1:3, 4   ❏ 1:3-7   ❏ 1:6   ❏ 1:19

3 What was so harmful about the false doctrines that were being taught in Ephesus?

_____

_____

_____

_____

4 What did Paul mean by "wholesome teaching" (1:10)?

_____

_____

_____

5 Why could Paul's word and opinion be trusted above those of the false teachers?

_____

_____

_____

This chapter contrasts the heretical doctrine of the false teachers with the right teaching of Paul. Sound teaching forms a solid foundation for faith; without a firm foundation, the building crumbles. The situation in Ephesus was critical because people in the church were being led away from the faith. Paul wanted Timothy to put a stop to the false teaching and to command certain men not to teach anymore. This was especially critical in churches such as Ephesus, where many of the believers were Gentiles with little or no knowledge about the Old Testament. In this setting it was relatively easy for new, destructive heresies to spread and take hold. Like Timothy, we must carefully examine what is taught. This is not just an academic matter, because what we believe directly influences how we live. Because we live in a time when truth is considered relative and people are led by their feelings rather than by their thoughts, we must take added precautions to preserve wholesome teaching, keeping our faith-foundation strong.

REALIZE
the principle

6 What are some of the avenues that allow false teaching to enter a church today?

_____

_____

_____

7 What does your church or denomination do to preserve wholesome teaching?

_____

_____

_____

8 How should churches oversee what is taught to children and teenagers in Sunday school and other programs?

_____

_____

_____

9 How might teachers in church be screened?

_____

_____

10 How can you determine what are major issues (which must be carefully guarded) and what are minor issues (where there is room for a variety of opinions and interpretations)?

_____

_____

_____

11 How can a church ensure wholesome teaching while allowing freedom for discussion, questions, and disagreements?

_____

_____

_____

RESPOND
to the message

12 When might disagreement be needed and useful in the church today? How can we avoid dangerous or pointless controversies?

_____

_____

_____

_____

13 What do you see as your role in preserving sound teaching in your church?

_____

_____

_____

14 How can you know if your opinions, beliefs, and interpretation of Scripture are going off in a heretical direction?

_____

_____

_____

15 What can you do to protect yourself from false teachers and false teaching?

_____

_____

_____

16 Where can you go for answers if you have questions regarding teaching?

_____

_____

17 Each of us needs a teaching check from time to time to make sure we have not unintentionally strayed from the truth. What teachings do you need to review? About what are you interested in learning more?

_____

_____

_____

_____

18 Make a list of questions you have regarding your faith or other aspects of the Bible or theology. (No one is sure about everything.) Then set up an appointment with your pastor or a knowledgeable friend for a checkup on your teaching.

RESOLVE
to take action

_____

_____

_____

_____

A What did Paul mean when he called Timothy his "true son in the faith" (1:2)? Who might be considered your spiritual parents? your spiritual children?

MORE
for studying
other themes
in this section

B What is the proper use of the law for us today? How might we use it improperly?

C How did the motivation of the false teachers (1:7) differ from the motivation of Paul (1:12)? What motivates you to teach others?

D How did Paul live a righteous life? Why then does he call himself the worst of sinners (1:15)? How did Paul's attitude help him minister to others?

E What do we learn about the character of God the Father from the doxology in 1:17? If you were writing a song of praise to God, what attributes would you list?

F How could a person shipwreck his or her faith?

G What did Hymenaeus and Alexander do? What does their punishment teach us about church discipline?

LESSON 3
THE CENTRALITY OF PRAYER
1 TIMOTHY 2:1-15

REFLECT
on your life

1 Think through your most recent worship service at church. List the times of prayer you can remember.

_____

_____

_____

2 Why do some prayers seem too long or make your mind wander?

_____

_____

_____

READ
the passage

Read 1 Timothy 2:1-15 and the following notes:

❒ 2:1-4   ❒ 2:2   ❒ 2:8

3 In 2:1 Paul tells us to "pray for all people. . . . Intercede on their behalf." How can we prepare ourselves to pray more effectively?

_____

_____

_____

_____

4 What does Paul say is good and pleasing to God?

_____

_____

_____

Prayer should be central to our life and our public worship. In this chapter Paul says he wants everyone to pray (2:8), and he urges that prayer be made for everyone (2:1). This means that we should not exempt any believer from praying nor exclude anyone from our prayers. Sometimes we let our mind wander while praying in church or regard public prayer as only a ceremony. After all, we may not know the people mentioned in the prayers. If asked what we enjoy in church, many would mention the opportunity to sing, listen to the sermon, and fellowship with other believers. Few would say they look forward to the long prayers. Yet prayer is a vital part of our worship. Those who live in religiously restricted countries certainly value prayer more highly than we do. Let prayer become your focus of attention over the next few weeks so that you can bring your attitude more in line with Paul's advice to Timothy.

REALIZE
the principle

5 Why is personal prayer alone insufficient? Why should believers be involved in corporate prayer as well?

_____

_____

_____

6 Why is it difficult to explain to young people the importance of prayer during worship services?

_____

_____

_____

_____

7 What dangerous consequences might there be for a church that spends little or no time in corporate prayer?

_____

_____

_____

_____

8 How might your attitude toward prayer in worship change if corporate prayer was restricted by law to Sunday mornings?

RESPOND
to the message

_____

_____

_____

_____

9 What should be the purpose of prayer in our worship? What should be our attitude as we pray?

_____

_____

_____

10 Paul says that we should pray for everyone. How can we expand the scope of our prayers?

_____

_____

_____

11 What does it mean to pray without "anger and controversy" (2:8)? How do we violate this guideline?

_____

_____

_____

12 How can we unintentionally degrade or demean our corporate prayer? How do we lift up unholy hands in prayer today?

_____

_____

_____

13 What are some of the reasons why it is difficult to pray for the government and those in authority over us? For whom do you often neglect to pray?

_____

_____

_____

_____

14 For which world leaders might it be difficult for you to pray? For whom or what do you avoid praying?

_____

_____

_____

15 What do you usually think about when your mind wanders during prayer in church? How can you focus your attention and join in the prayer completely?

_____

_____

_____

_____

16 What practical steps can you take to participate more wholeheartedly in times of corporate prayer? How can you make prayer a more meaningful aspect of your weekly worship?

RESOLVE
to take action

_____

_____

_____

_____

_____

A What does it mean that God "wants everyone to be saved and to understand the truth" (2:4)? What implications does this have on our evangelistic efforts?

MORE
for studying
other themes
in this section

B Why is having only one Mediator important (2:5)? Why was this significant at the time this letter was written?

C What does it mean to be modest in appearance in a time of changing tastes, fashions, and sensibilities? Why is dressing modestly so important?

D How do we make ourselves attractive by the good things we do? How does this apply to men as well?

E What does it mean for us to learn quietly and submissively?

F Why were women not permitted to teach? What does this mean for us today?

G What does it mean that "women will be saved through childbearing" (2:15)? How should we understand this verse?

H How does a person continue in "faith, love, holiness, and modesty" (2:15)?

LESSON 4
THE TRAINING GROUND
FOR CHURCH LEADERS
1 TIMOTHY 3:1-16

REFLECT
on your life

1 Some people learn their working skills on the job; others learn their skills at school. Where did you receive the training you needed for your current job or role?

_____

_____

_____

2 Describe one of the best learning experiences that you can remember. What made it so effective for you?

_____

_____

_____

_____

_____

READ
the passage

Read 1 Timothy 3:1-16 and the following notes:

❐ 3:1 ❐ 3:1-13 ❐ 3:2 ❐ 3:4, 5 ❐ 3:8-13

3 What is the difference between an elder and a deacon? How do these positions correspond to categories of responsibility in your church?

_____

_____

4 What does it mean to be able to manage your children and household well?

_____

_____

_____

The family is a training class and proving ground for leaders in the church. Much can be determined about an individual's fitness to lead in church by finding out how he or she behaves at home. How we behave at home tells others much about our character and conduct. Our spouse, children, and relatives can provide feedback and encouragement to improve our character and conduct. Home is a proving ground because we must demonstrate the skills for leading the church by effectively leading our own families. Because the church is God's family, those who set their hearts on leadership should start at home. Those who are heavily involved in the church should never neglect their family responsibilities.

REALIZE
the principle

5 What are the qualifications for becoming a leader in your church? How are new leaders selected? How are they trained?

_____

_____

_____

6 What might be the consequences for a congregation that elects leaders who have not managed their own families well?

_____

_____

_____

_____

7 Why is wanting to become an elder considered an "honorable" desire (3:1)? When would it be wrong to set your heart on becoming a leader in your church?

RESPOND
to the message

_____

_____

_____

_____

8 Explain what each of the following qualifications means today:

Above reproach: _____

Faithful to his wife: _____

Exercises self-control: _____

Lives wisely: _____

Has a good reputation: _____

Enjoys having guests in his home: _____

Able to teach: _____

Not a heavy drinker: _____

Not violent but gentle: _____

Not quarrelsome: _____

Not one who loves money: _____

Manages his own family well: _____

His children respect and obey him: _____

Not a new believer: _____

People outside the church must speak well of him: _____

9 Which of these qualifications might be a problem for you?

_____

_____

_____

10 Though all believers should strive to meet these qualifications, why is it especially important that church leaders meet them?

_____

_____

11 What are some of the most important aspects of managing one's family well?

_____

_____

_____

12 How has your home life shaped your character?

_____

_____

_____

13 What can those who are single or who have no family do to prepare themselves for leadership in the church?

_____

_____

14 In what ways are you a leader in your church right now? How would you like to lead in ten or twenty years?

_____

_____

_____

15 What flaws in your character or conduct have been exposed in your home and need attention? How can your marriage and family life most help and strengthen you to lead in the church?

_____

_____

_____

_____

_____

16 Review the way you act at home. How are you falling short of the standards presented in this chapter? What lessons do you need to learn that you have been putting off or resisting?

RESOLVE
to take action

_____

_____

_____

_____

_____

A How does the ability to manage one's household relate to being a leader at church? How does managing a home differ from managing at work?

MORE
for studying
other themes
in this section

B What does it mean that deacons should be closely examined before being appointed (3:10)? How does your church examine those who aspire to leadership?

C Why was it important to teach people how to conduct themselves in the household of faith? What are some mistakes in conduct that we could easily make today?

D What is the "great mystery of our faith" (3:16)?

E How does the hymn in 3:16 refute the heresy that was affecting the believers in Ephesus? Which of these statements about Christ does your church need to emphasize?

LESSON 5
THE POWER OF A GOOD EXAMPLE
1 TIMOTHY 4:1-16

REFLECT
on your life

1 Describe a person who has had a powerful influence on your life. Why did his or her example speak louder than words?

_____

_____

_____

_____

_____

2 When has your life had a strong impact on someone else, positively or negatively?

_____

_____

_____

READ
the passage

Read 1 Timothy 4:1-16 and the following notes:

❏ 4:7-10   ❏ 4:12   ❏ 4:14   ❏ 4:16

3 What is godliness?

_____

_____

_____

4 How does a person train to be godly (4:7)?

_____

_____

_____

5 What is the benefit of watching yourself closely and setting a good example (4:16)?

_____

_____

_____

_____

Paul told Timothy to train himself to be godly (4:7), to be an example for the believers (4:12), and to watch his life and teaching closely (4:16). He was to be a living example of what he was teaching. Living God's way still provides a powerful example today, and our influence is multiplied when what we do is reinforced by what we say. In church, our words will not be neutralized by our actions. Outside the church, no one will be able to criticize us. How we live speaks louder than what we say. What kind of example will you set?

REALIZE
the principle

6 How do we keep a close watch on our conduct without becoming self-conscious in all we do?

_____

_____

_____

_____

7 In what situations do you feel put down because of your age, education, or position?

RESPOND
to the message

_____

_____

_____

_____

8 What are some specific ways to set good examples for other believers . . .

in what you teach? _____

_____

_____

in the way you live? _____

_____

_____

in your love? _____

_____

_____

in your faith? _____

_____

_____

in your purity? _____

_____

_____

9 How would you rate yourself as an example in each of the areas that Paul indicated to Timothy?

Life area	Good		Needs improvement		Poor
Teaching	5	4	3	2	1
Life	5	4	3	2	1
Love	5	4	3	2	1
Faith	5	4	3	2	1
Purity	5	4	3	2	1

10 Which of the above areas is most important for you to begin taking action in right now?

_____

_____

_____

_____

_____

11 As you watch your life and teaching more closely, what might interfere with making the necessary changes?

_____

_____

_____

_____

_____

12 Select one area of your life to improve. How can you be diligent and persevere in this area? What will it mean to submit yourself to training for godliness in
this area?

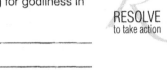

RESOLVE
to take action

_____

_____

_____

_____

_____

A How do deceptive spirits cause people to turn away from their faith today?

MORE
for studying
other themes
in this section

B How does a conscience become dead (4:2)? What hope is there for someone
who has not kept a good conscience?

C How can we tell when it is best to keep our thoughts to ourselves and when
we should confront others (4:6)?

D Why are people often more concerned about physical fitness than about
spiritual fitness?

E What are some of the alternatives to placing our hope in God?

F What should be the role of reading Scripture in the church today? How could
it be more effective?

G What should be the primary duties of a pastor? How does your church help
your pastor to meet these duties?

H How are you gifted? What gift are you in danger of neglecting?

I What is the value of others seeing our faith-progress? How does this compare
with not flaunting our good works?

LESSON 6
RESPECT IN RELATIONSHIPS
1 TIMOTHY 5:1–6:2a

REFLECT
on your life

1 Describe a time when someone from church did not treat you very well. How did you feel?

_____

_____

_____

2 Think of times in your life when someone treated you respectfully. What was done that made you feel respected?

_____

_____

_____

_____

READ
the passage

Read 1 Timothy 5:1–6:2a and the following notes:

❒ 5:2   ❒ 5:3-5   ❒ 5:8   ❒ 5:19-21   ❒ 5:21   ❒ 6:1, 2

3 Why do we need the same advice that Paul gave Timothy about how to treat various kinds of people?

_____

_____

4 What were the apparent abuses and problems in the way the church dealt with widows?

_____

_____

_____

5 Why would a Christian slave be tempted to disrespect his or her Christian master?

_____

_____

_____

Timothy was to treat people in the church with the same level of respect as he would his own family. No matter what our age or place in life, we should treat others in the church as we would fathers, brothers, mothers, or sisters. But often we treat a waitress or service attendant more courteously than we do our spouse. And we often treat casual acquaintances with more decency than our own brothers and sisters. Similarly, we often treat our brothers and sisters in Christ as though they were less than members of God's family. We need wisdom in our relationships. Older and younger people need to be treated differently, yet all should be treated with dignity. We do this by showing respect without partiality. We should make an effort to treat everybody in the church with respect. After all, these people will be with us for eternity.

REALIZE
the principle

6 Paul mentioned the older and younger men, the older and younger women, widows, elders, and slaves. Describe the different kinds of people in your church.

_____

_____

_____

_____

_____

7 How do some of these people (the old, the young, the poor) become invisible to others in the church?

_____

_____

_____

_____

8 What are some of the benefits of having people of various ages in the body of Christ?

_____

_____

_____

_____

9 How can we show our respect for elders in the congregation without being phony or superficial?

_____

_____

_____

10 How can we unintentionally show favoritism in the church?

_____

_____

_____

11 What should you do to show your employer full respect? How might lack of respect for your employer hinder your testimony or give Christians a bad name?

_____

_____

_____

_____

12 What might be especially difficult about attending the same church as someone from your place of work?

_____

_____

_____

13 With what kind of people in your church do you feel most comfortable? With what age or background of people do you relate the best?

_____

_____

_____

14 With which type of people in the church do you feel uncomfortable or avoid contact?

_____

_____

_____

15 When do you have problems showing respect to others in the body of Christ? How do you play favorites?

_____

_____

_____

16 Evaluate your relationships in church. What can you do to improve how you relate to certain types of people? What can you do to strengthen intergenerational ties? What can you do to become more aware of the less visible people?

RESOLVE
to take action

_____

_____

_____

_____

A Why is it important for a younger person not to speak harshly to an older person?

MORE
for studying
other themes
in this section

B What does it mean for men to treat younger women with purity?

C What should a church do about a parent who is not being taken care of by his or her children? When is it time for the church to step in?

D In what way does taking care of parents as they age repay them?

E What was difficult about the plight of widows at the time of this letter? Why did these widows have to qualify for financial help? How did the younger widows become "guilty of breaking their previous pledge" (5:12)? Why was this a problem?

F What are some opportunities for helping those in our own families who are in need? How much time might it take? What are possible complications? How much personal and financial sacrifice might this mandate?

G Why should pastors be paid for their efforts?

H What could make people accuse elders of wrongdoing?

I Why is it so difficult for us to rebuke publicly those who sin today? How could this be carried out inappropriately? What was the intention of this directive?

J Why do good deeds stand out so much? What good have you done that has not stood out? What do you do that nobody else seems to notice?

LESSON 7
FOR THE LOVE OF MONEY
1 TIMOTHY 6:2b-21

REFLECT
on your life

1 If you could take any of your possessions with you to heaven, what would you like to take? Why?

_____

_____

_____

_____

2 How can you tell if someone loves money?

_____

_____

_____

READ
the passage

Read 1 Timothy 6:2b-21 and the following notes:

❏ 6:3-5   ❏ 6:6   ❏ 6:6-10   ❏ 6:8, 9   ❏ 6:11, 12   ❏ 6:17-19

3 What is the connection between false teaching and desire for financial gain?

_____

_____

_____

4 How did Paul recommend that Timothy deal with the temptation to love money?

_____

_____

_____

5 How can wealth be a problem for a Christian?

_____

_____

_____

_____

What is so attractive about wealth that we will sacrifice the rest of our life to get it? What is it about money that makes it so addictive? Why is it so difficult to realize when we are being caught up by the love of money? Wanting to be rich or wanting to have more is not just a disease of the wealthy. So beware if you think you do not have to worry about greed because you are in debt rather than wealthy. You may still love money even though you have not stockpiled much of it. The problem is not how much money you have but how badly you want it. It is the love of money that is a root of all kinds of evil, and keeping our heart weeded of this root proves more difficult than we may think. Most people want more money, and few would turn down an opportunity to make some quick cash. We must carefully consider our desires and keep our priorities straight, because wanting more money can lead to many kinds of sin.

REALIZE
the principle

6 What is the danger of wanting to get rich? What impact does this desire have on personal faith? on family? on church involvement? on relationships?

_____

_____

_____

_____

_____

7 To what extent do the people in your church seem to love money?

_____

_____

_____

8 How can we learn to be content with what we have? Why is this so difficult?

_____

_____

_____

RESPOND
to the message

9 What techniques have you used to help curb your desire for wealth?

_____

_____

_____

_____

10 Why is it difficult to live on less than you earn? What guidelines do you use to make major spending decisions?

_____

_____

_____

_____

_____

11 When is the desire for more money sinful or unhealthy? When is it right for you to want more money?

_____

_____

_____

_____

12 What is it that drives you to want more money? What is it that will free you from these desires?

_____

_____

_____

_____

_____

13 What are you doing that is primarily fueled and driven by the love of money? What would you stop doing if it were not for the love of money?

_____

_____

_____

_____

14 What would happen if you decided to be content with what you have? What would happen if you decided to try to live on less? How difficult would this be for you to do? What barriers would you face in attempting this?

_____

_____

_____

_____

_____

15 What would it take to get rid of your love of money? What practical steps can you take now to start the process?

RESOLVE
to take action

_____

_____

_____

_____

_____

A How can the love of money weaken your faith?

B What does it mean to "fight the good fight" for what we believe (6:12)? How do we "hold tightly" to eternal life?

C How can we warn those who are rich not to put their hope in their riches? How can we get them to listen to us without suspicion? How wealthy do you have to be before this warning applies to you?

D How hard would it be for you to say no to an opportunity for additional income? What criteria would you use for making that decision?

E Why is it so difficult to be generous and give our money away even though we may have more than enough on which to live?

F How do we store up treasure in heaven?

MORE
for studying
other themes
in this section

LESSON 8
CHRISTIAN CHARACTER IN A CORRUPT WORLD
TITUS 1:1-16

REFLECT
on your life

1 What comes to your mind when you hear the words *chaos* and *mess*?

_____

_____

_____

2 Think of a time when you had to straighten out a mess. How did you go about organizing and restoring order?

_____

_____

3 Think of a time when you were asked to complete something left unfinished. What were your feelings as you started the task?

_____

_____

READ
the passage

Read the introduction to Titus, Titus 1:1-16, and the following notes:

❑ 1:1　❑ 1:2　❑ 1:5　❑ 1:5-9　❑ 1:15

4 Why did Paul ask Titus to go to Crete?

_____

_____

5 Why was it important for the elders to be well versed in trustworthy teaching?

_____

_____

6 Why was it important to silence those who rebelled against right teaching?

_____

_____

Paul told Titus to appoint elders and to silence false teachers. He was to build up the muscle of, and remove the cancer from, the church in Crete. For Titus to complete this difficult task, he had to select leaders of the highest moral integrity. Character is just as important for leaders and followers in churches today. Like the believers in Crete, we live in a corrupt world that wars against the development of strong character. The significance of solid Christian character should always be emphasized in our life. Work diligently and pray fervently to ensure the development of your character. Encourage others not to be sidetracked or hindered by the world around them. Select leaders cautiously so that your church will be known for developing Christians with strong character.

REALIZE
the principle

7 What is God's role in the development of sound Christian character?

_____

_____

_____

8 What are the similarities and differences between the churches at Crete and our churches today?

_____

_____

_____

_____

_____

_____

9 Each of the qualifications mentioned by Paul reveals something about a person's character. Explain why each one is important for a church leader.

RESPOND
to the message

A blameless life: _____

Faithful to his wife: _____

Believing children: _____

Obedient children: _____

Not arrogant: _____

Not quick-tempered: _____

Not a heavy drinker: _____

Not violent: _____

Not dishonest with money: _____

Hospitable: _____

Loves good: _____

Fair: _____

Devout: _____

Disciplined: _____

Strong and steadfast belief: _____

Able to encourage and correct others: _____

10 Review the previous list. Which aspects of your character need the most attention?

_____

_____

_____

11 What are some reasons why character development is difficult?

_____

_____

_____

12 Which of your goals for life are related to the development of your character?

_____

_____

_____

13 In which areas of your character has the Holy Spirit been working lately? In what areas would you like God's help?

_____

_____

_____

_____

14 In what ways would you like to have a stronger character in five years?

_____

_____

_____

15 Set a goal for the development of a specific aspect of your character. What would be some concrete milestones to mark your progress? What are some immediate steps for getting started on this?

RESOLVE
to take action

_____

_____

_____

_____

_____

_____

A How does knowing the truth help one to live a godly life?

B What does it mean to be blameless in our society today?

C How are we able to encourage others with right teaching? Why is it important to be able to show those who oppose it where they are wrong?

D What were the advocates of circumcision doing that was so destructive to the faith of the believers? Who in our society is trying to destroy faith? How can we oppose them and their efforts?

E How do lying, cruelty, and laziness manifest themselves in our society today?

F When is it right to rebuke others sternly, and when is it out of place? How should we handle those in the church who are teaching what is not right?

G How can everything be pure to those whose hearts are pure when there is so much evil in the world?

H How could a Christian make himself or herself "worthless for doing anything good" (1:16)? What happens when this person disqualifies himself or herself for service?

MORE
for studying
other themes
in this section

LESSON 9
LEARNING A NEW WAY OF LIFE
TITUS 2:1-15

REFLECT
on your life

1 What rich and famous people do you find the most objectionable? What do their lifestyles tell you about their values?

_____

_____

_____

_____

2 Who comes to mind as a good model of a person living a Christian lifestyle? What about this person impresses you the most?

_____

_____

_____

_____

READ
the passage

Read Titus 2:1-15 and the following notes:

❐ 2:2-8   ❐ 2:2, 5   ❐ 2:6   ❐ 2:7, 8   ❐ 2:8   ❐ 2:9, 10   ❐ 2:15

3 What groups are listed in this section? Why are the directives to each group different?

_____

_____

_____

4 How can behavior in the home bring shame on the word of God?

_____

_____

_____

_____

5 How can our behavior "make the teaching about God our Savior attractive" (2:10)?

_____

_____

_____

Titus had a difficult task in helping believers learn how to live for Christ in a hostile environment. In this chapter, Paul gives pointed advice to various groups in the church. The older men were to be worthy of respect, the older women were to live godly lives. The young women were to be pure, and the young men were "to live wisely" (2:6). Titus was to be a model for them. To teach others how to live as a Christian still requires teachers who live what is being taught. Christian living does not come from mere self-effort, peer pressure, or regulations within the church. Someone must teach people how to do it. What is your role in teaching the Christian lifestyle to various groups? You may not have time to be involved in church as much as you would like, but you do have time to demonstrate how to live faithfully in a hostile environment. No matter where you are in life or what your position is, you have no excuse for poor character and an undisciplined lifestyle.

REALIZE
the principle

6 What are some of the implications regarding Christian education in the church that we can draw from this chapter?

_____

_____

_____

7 What aspects of Christian lifestyle should be taught in church today? What specific guidelines would be most appropriate for each of the various groups?

_____

_____

_____

_____

_____

8 What is the importance of living a pure life? What makes this especially challenging in our time and culture?

_____

_____

_____

_____

9 How do the older people train the younger people in your church? What opportunities do you have to learn from those who are older? What opportunities do you have to teach those who are younger?

_____

_____

_____

_____

10 How did you learn how to be faithful to Christ? Who was your "Paul"?

_____

_____

_____

11 Who have you tried to teach about living a Christian lifestyle? What have been the results? What did you do well? What would you do differently?

_____

_____

_____

_____

_____

12 In which of the groups that Paul mentions would you place yourself? How would you evaluate your own performance of the qualities listed for that group?

_____

_____

_____

_____

13 What key area of your lifestyle do you need to work on most right now?

RESOLVE
to take action

_____

_____

_____

_____

_____

14 What could you do to make substantial progress right away? How could you spend more time with someone who would be a good model for you? To what other resources could you turn for help?

_____

_____

_____

_____

A Why is it important for young men to live wisely in all they do?

B Why was it important for Titus's teaching to be beyond criticism? How can teachers in the church today maintain the highest level of integrity in their teaching?

C What can employees do to make the teaching about God attractive? What roles do honesty and integrity play in this?

D What kinds of precautions should we take to live a pure life?

E What was the importance of teaching the slaves who were believers to make an effort to please their masters? What are some parallels for us?

MORE
for studying
other themes
in this section

LESSON 10
DEVOTED TO DOING GOOD
TITUS 3:1-15

REFLECT
on your life

1 Think back to one of the first times you fully devoted yourself to a sport, a job, or a person. What did this devotion cost you? What did you gain?

_____

_____

_____

_____

2 Think of someone you know who is truly devoted to something. What does this person do or say that shows his or her devotion?

_____

_____

_____

READ
the passage

Read Titus 3:1-15 and the following notes:

❑ 3:1   ❑ 3:3   ❑ 3:4-8   ❑ 3:4-6

3 What does it mean to be "always ready to do what is good" (3:1)?

_____

_____

_____

4 What does it mean to do good (3:8)?

_____

_____

_____

5 On what basis does Christ save us (3:5)?

_____

_____

_____

REALIZE
the principle

In this chapter Paul makes it clear to Titus that he wants believers to devote themselves to doing what is good (3:1, 8, 14). We, too, should devote ourselves to doing what is good. But where do we find the motivation on days when we just don't feel like it? The devotion Paul speaks of does not come from working to please someone. It springs out of thankfulness for what God has done for us. If we remind ourselves that we were once disobedient and that we have been justified by God's grace, then we will want to serve God because we are so grateful. This deep gratitude gives us the motivation to do good on the days we are tired or preoccupied. God's forgiveness sets us free to devote ourselves to doing what is good.

6 Other than their love for God, what are some motives people have for doing good? What is wrong with these motives?

_____

_____

_____

_____

7 Why do so many believers still try to earn God's approval by doing good rather than doing good as a response to what he has already done for them?

_____

_____

_____

8 How would you describe your devotion to doing good? Place an *X* on the appropriate step.

perfectly devoted
wholeheartedly devoted
thoroughly devoted
fully devoted
adequately devoted
usually devoted
often devoted
somewhat devoted
slightly devoted
occasionally devoted
not really devoted

RESPOND
to the message

9 What would it take to get you to move up another step or two in your level of devotion?

_____

_____

10 Where are the trouble spots in your devotion to doing good? When do you begin to feel your devotion sag?

_____

_____

_____

11 What are the barriers you face in devoting yourself to doing good? What seems unpleasant about this? What holds you back from wanting to be more devoted?

_____

_____

12 What would bolster your devotion and your ability to do good?

_____

_____

13 What changes could you make to better prepare yourself to do what is good?

_____

_____

_____

14 How are you doing harm to others? What can you stop doing that would result in good?

_____

_____

_____

15 If you are not devoting your life to doing good, to what are you devoting it?

_____

_____

_____

16 How do you balance doing good for others with all of the other responsibilities in your life? When can doing good for others get in the way of providing for your family or being responsible at work?

_____

_____

_____

_____

_____

17 What are some good things you could do this week? To which good causes could you devote yourself or increase your level of commitment? Who could you be more ready to serve or help out? How could you begin to put your increased level of devotion to work?

RESOLVE
to take action

_____

_____

_____

_____

_____

_____

_____

_____

A Why is it important to submit to the government? What happens when we are not obedient?

MORE
for studying
other themes
in this section

B What does it mean to be "slaves to many lusts and pleasures" (3:3)? How is a person set free from these traps?

C What kinds of discussions should you avoid? What are their dangers? When is it good and right to take a stand?

D Why is a divisive person such a threat to a church? How does being divisive differ from rebuking or being prophetic about an issue or situation?

E How would the church help Zenas and Apollos with their trip (3:13)? How can you help traveling Christian workers?

F What is so bad about living an unproductive life today? Does this mean we must be financial successes? What is a productive life? How can you be productive?

LESSON 11
SERVICE WITH A SMILE
2 TIMOTHY 1:1–2:26

REFLECT
on your life

1 Describe what you would consider to be superior service in a restaurant.

_____

_____

_____

_____

2 What do you appreciate most about those who provide good service?

_____

_____

_____

READ
the passage

Read the two-page introduction to 2 Timothy, 2 Timothy 1:1–2:26, and the following notes:

❐ 1:6   ❐ 1:6, 7   ❐ 1:7   ❐ 2:3-7   ❐ 2:15   ❐ 2:16   ❐ 2:20, 21

3 How is the main message of this letter different from that of 1 Timothy?

_____

_____

_____

4 How would you describe the relationship between Paul and Timothy? With whom do you have a similar relationship?

_____

_____

_____

_____

5 How can you make yourself "ready for the Master to use you for every good work" (2:21)?

_____

_____

_____

In these two chapters, Paul describes many of the characteristics of the servant who wins God's approval. A servant performs what is expected of him or her. A servant who is faithful and serves well earns special approval. Not only does this servant render superior service when asked, but this servant prepares him- or herself in order to always be ready to do the best job for the master. Paul's practical advice instructs anyone who wants to learn to serve God well: be strong through the grace that God gives you (2:1); endure suffering (2:3); remember Christ's incarnation and resurrection (2:8); correctly explain the word of truth (2:15); avoid worthless, foolish talk (2:16); keep yourself pure (2:21); pursue righteous living (2:22); and do not quarrel (2:24)—to mention a few. These guidelines are practical, yet provocative. They take a lifetime to master, yet we can practice them any day. These serve as practical guidelines for all who one day want to hear the words, "Well done, my good and faithful servant" (Matt 25:21).

REALIZE
the principle

6 Why is it important to learn to endure suffering in Christian service?

_____

_____

_____

_____

7 How are excellent employees in a service business similar to faithful servants of God? Why is this a helpful illustration for us?

_____

_____

_____

_____

8 What is your motivation for Christian service?

RESPOND
to the message

_____

_____

_____

9 What excites you most about the opportunity to serve God and others?

_____

_____

_____

10 What bothers you most about the idea of lifelong, faithful Christian service?

_____

_____

_____

11 List all of Paul's directives in these two chapters that are meaningful and helpful to you in learning how to be a better servant of God:

Verse	What Paul said	Why it is important for me

12 Which of these directives is most difficult for you to carry out? Which most urgently needs your attention and prayer?

_____

_____

_____

_____

13 What hinders your faithful Christian service?

_____

_____

14 Take the list in question 11 and turn it into a one-week training program for yourself. What can you do this week to better prepare yourself for God's service (for example, read books, make appointments, etc.)?

RESOLVE
to take action

_____

_____

_____

_____

_____

A Second Timothy was the last book in the New Testament that Paul wrote. Why is this fact important to us?

MORE
for studying
other themes
in this section

B What did Paul mean when he said he was an apostle by God's will? How does God affect your purpose in life?

C What is the "grace, mercy, and peace" that comes from God (1:2)?

D How can God help us overcome our fear of people?

E What is significant about the fact that we have done nothing to earn salvation? Why is it impossible for us to earn salvation?

F What is the difference between a "preacher, an apostle, and a teacher" (1:11)? How would you describe your special role in the Christian ministry?

G How can we learn to "be strong through the grace that God gives" us in Christ Jesus (2:1)?

H Why do you think 2 Timothy 2:2 is used to teach the discipleship process? Who are you discipling?

I In this day and age, how can we learn to endure suffering? How are a soldier, an athlete, and a farmer similar? Why did Paul use these examples?

J What is the distinction between fighting over words and making important distinctions? How do we avoid useless arguments?

K How do we correctly explain the word of truth? How do some misrepresent it?

L How do we learn to teach others gently? What sensitivities and skills does this task require?

LESSON 12
SPIRITUAL ENDURANCE
2 TIMOTHY 3:1–4:22

1 Think of a time in your life when your physical or emotional endurance was tested. What was it that kept you going?

REFLECT
on your life

_____

_____

_____

_____

2 When did you last have to increase your level of physical fitness for a sport or an activity? Why was physical endurance important for this?

_____

_____

_____

_____

Read 2 Timothy 3:1–4:22 and the following notes:

❑ 3:1ff ❑ 3:5 ❑ 3:9 ❑ 3:12 ❑ 3:14 ❑ 4:2 ❑ 4:5 ❑ 4:6-8 ❑ 4:18 ❑ 4:22

READ
the passage

3 Why will all who live a godly life suffer persecution (3:12)? What did Paul know about the times and the hearts of people? In what ways do we face persecution today?

_____

_____

_____

_____

4 Summarize the charge that Paul gave to Timothy (4:2). How can Christians be prepared whether the time is favorable or not?

_____

_____

_____

5 What will receiving a "crown of righteousness" signify (4:8)?

_____

_____

_____

Life was not becoming easier or more comfortable for Paul as he grew older. He was facing death, and believers in the cities to which he had brought the gospel were facing increased persecution. As he looked ahead, he clearly saw the importance of endurance. Paul wanted Timothy to remain faithful to what he had been taught (3:14), stick to the authority of the Scripture (3:16), encourage others with good teaching (4:2), not fear suffering (4:5), and complete his ministry (4:5). During difficult times, faith demands stick-to-itiveness. Faith that falls apart in tough times is of little use. Faith that fades over time will not help you in life, not to mention death. A steady flame is more useful for cooking than a flame that quickly ignites and then sputters. Will the flame of your faith flicker or burn brighter over time? Like Paul and Timothy, we may encounter more difficulties in living for Christ as we grow older. Each year we will face new challenges to our faith that require endurance. Ask God for endurance during the difficult days ahead.

REALIZE
the principle

6 How does our society make it difficult for us to live out our faith?

_____

_____

_____

_____

7 What is difficult about remaining true to Christ as we grow older? What makes it easier to continue in our faith?

_____

_____

_____

_____

8 What role can the Bible play in developing our spiritual endurance?

_____

_____

_____

_____

9 Comparing your faith to a campfire, would you say your faith has just ignited, is burning brightly, is slowing down, or is smoldering?

_____

_____

_____

_____

10 How might living a Christian life be easier for you ten years from now? How might it be more difficult?

_____

_____

_____

_____

_____

11 What do you need to remove from your life that may drain your strength and weaken your ability to endure?

_____

_____

_____

_____

12 How can the Bible help you to be thoroughly equipped for a lifetime of service to Christ? What kind of study program would be most beneficial for you?

_____

_____

_____

_____

13 How can you improve your spiritual endurance? What steps do you need to take to get your faith in shape?

RESOLVE
to take action

_____

_____

_____

_____

_____

A Look at the list of sins in 3:2-5. Which of these describes your community? your society? What has been on the news recently that illustrates what Paul is saying?

MORE
for studying
other themes
in this section

B What does 4:1 tell us about the authority of Jesus? How should his authority motivate us to live?

C Why was Paul warning that some will no longer listen to sound teaching? Why do some people today find it so easy to reject sound teaching?

D What was Paul's purpose for living? How did it affect the way he lived? Compare this to your purpose and lifestyle.

E What kinds of persecutions did Paul endure in his lifetime? What are some of the persecutions that believers are facing throughout the world at this time? How do you endure persecution?

F What does it mean that all Scripture is inspired by God? What difference does this make in your own study and interpretation of the Bible?

LESSON 13
FINDING COURAGE TO FACE CHALLENGES
TIMOTHY CONCLUSION

REFLECT
on your life

1 Describe a person who has been a mentor to you at school, at work, or at church.

_____

_____

_____

_____

2 What life experiences have specially prepared you to serve God?

_____

_____

_____

_____

READ
the passage

Read Timothy's profile found in 1 Timothy.

3 What did Timothy have going for him and against him in his work as a missionary?

_____

_____

_____

4 How did Timothy's family background prepare him for service? How has your family background specially prepared you for serving God?

_____

_____

_____

5 What were Timothy's weaknesses? How did these tend to impede his ministry?

_____

_____

_____

_____

Timothy was a Gentile who was intimately familiar with the Old Testament and Christianity. God had specially prepared Timothy for a life of service to him through a strong Christian mother. Later, Timothy joined Paul as a fellow mis- sionary. He was close to the leading missionaries for the entire Greek-speaking world, and yet he still felt awkward around those who were older. All of us have insecurities that make certain tasks more difficult for us. Even the best educa- tion and the most exciting experiences will not change everything about us. We will still continue to struggle with certain aspects of our personality. But Christ can give us the power to do what is difficult or seemingly impossible. Like Timothy, we can look to Christ for the courage to do what is needed and right.

REALIZE
the principle

6 What might Timothy have learned from his close association with Paul?

_____

_____

_____

7 How do you think these letters encouraged Timothy? How can they help and encourage us?

_____

_____

_____

_____

_____

8 Why does becoming a Christian not solve all our problems with personality and character?

_____

_____

_____

_____

9 Who has discipled you? Whom have you trained? Who has been a Paul in your life? Who has been a Timothy?

_____

_____

_____

_____

10 What does the friendship of Paul and Timothy teach us about the relationship of those who work together for the cause of Christ? What does this tell you about your relationships?

_____

_____

_____

_____

_____

11 Who has recognized your potential? What did they observe?

_____

_____

_____

_____

12 What fears or inabilities tend to get in the way of your service to God?

_____

_____

_____

_____

_____

13 In what situations do you feel that others look down on you? What can you do to prevent this from inhibiting your ministry?

_____

_____

_____

_____

14 What challenges are you currently facing that you believe are beyond your experience or ability?

_____

_____

_____

_____

_____

15 What is the most important lesson you have learned from Timothy that can help you face one of these challenges with more courage? What are some of the first steps you can take to put this into practice?

RESOLVE
to take action

_____

_____

_____

_____

_____

A Summarize the main message of each of the three books in this study. What is the significance of each book for today? What was the most helpful insight you gained from each?

MORE
for studying
other themes
in this section

B Look up all of the other verses mentioning Timothy in the Bible. Where did he travel? What other leaders in the early church did he apparently know? How do you think these experiences helped prepare him for leadership in the church? What is God using to prepare you?

C What is the significance of these three books for our understanding of the nature and function of the church? What are some of the insights that are meaningful as you think about your own church?

D Why is it important to teach the truths of the Bible to trustworthy people who will in turn pass them on to others (2 Tim 2:2)? How are you passing these truths on to others?

E Of the three books included in this study, which is your personal favorite? Which would you recommend to a friend? What is the most important lesson you have learned? What can you do to retain this knowledge and put it into practice?